Shazia Calvert-Davies was born in Karachi, Pakistan, in 1971. Her nomadic trail took her from a childhood in Kuwait to boarding school in England. Further education culminated in a bachelor of journalism from the US. Returning to London her advertising career spanned from Bartle Bogle Hegarty to Abbott Mead Vickers BBDO before joining Deutsch Inc., New York.

Many happily married years later, her role as a full-time wife and mother was brutally disturbed by breast cancer. Ironically, her journalism took a new turn. This time, documenting her journey back to life and raising funds for South Asian breast cancer, as an author.

In memory of my dearest friend, Maja Cederwell. September 16, 1970–November 7, 2017. You'll always be my "Whispering Angel".

Shazia Calvert-Davies

BREAST CANCER SMILES

Life Through a Different Lens

AUSTIN MACAULEY PUBLISHERS™

LONDON * CAMBRIDGE * NEW YORK * SHARJAH

A CIP catalogue record for this title is available from the British Library.

ISBN 9781528905701 (Paperback)
ISBN 9781528907767 (Hardback)
ISBN 9781528908429 (ePub e-book)

www.austinmacauley.com

First Published 2021
Austin Macauley Publishers Ltd®
1 Canada Square
Canary Wharf
London
E14 5AA

Jonathan, my husband
Thank you doesn't suffice. For carrying my heart and soul for 20 years. For the unconditional love, only blood is supposed to provide. For being the reason, I could smile through so much pain. For giving me the best years of my life.

Kameron and Kurran, our boys
Thank you. For pushing my boundaries and making me reach higher, to be a better Mum. I know this has been too hard for you to engage with. That understanding has enabled me to grow.

Abida, my mother
Thank you. For believing in me. You are the only parent that stepped up to the plate. The only parent I've known. You chose the road less travelled and pushed me through this thing called life.

Abba and Phupo, my Grandparents
Thank you. For the adoring eyes, the bursting pride and quite simply the love. I will always miss you.

Sadia Barlow Photography
Thank you. First to my sister, Sadia, for honouring the bond. Second, to the husband/wife duo that is Sadia Barlow Photography. For harnessing your talent and creativity behind

the lens, providing image after powerful image documenting my journey. All for the joy of furthering my campaign.

Jo Bassford and Sophie Evans, two amazing sisters-in-law.
Jo, thank you for all the support emotional and medical. You are one of the most instinctive doctors I have ever come across. Having the initial input from Jo added to the best medical team was simply my huge fortune. Sophie, for the love, the wonderful videos just to make me smile and your natural positive energy.

My medical team at The Royal Marsden Hospital, Chelsea and Sutton
Thank you. To Professor Stephen Johnston, Miss Fiona MacNeill, Mr Stuart James, Dr Anna Kirby, Dr Matthew Brown. I am blessed with what I call the "A team" in cancer care. A special mention to the breast care nurses, the Robert Tiffany Ward and the fantastic chemo nurses who are such unsung heroes. I am also deeply grateful for the excellence of The Royal Marsden Hospital. And to the lady in chemo reception, who always loved my handbags. You are the cutest.

Sir Nigel Bogle and Sir John Bartle of Bartle Bogle Hegarty
Thank you. For enabling the author in me years ago. For all your personal support through the IPA Effectiveness Awards and the belief in my writing that I never had. I will forever be indebted to you both and Sir John Hegarty for creating an environment where I could be so passionate about my job. I spent some of my best years working for Bartle Bogle Hegarty.

My Hurst Lodge Schoolgirls
Thank you. For being here since we were little girls. For being that group of women one can share happiness and true sadness

with. For sharing memories of some of us that is missing. Maja (one of us) and Ruby (one of our little ones) we love you and miss you.

Rachael Bland
Thank you. For responding to my note. For saying my "Insta" was amazing. For wanting to know more about my cause and the reasons why breast cancer was taboo in South Asia. For giving me so much strength without even knowing your power on the day of my surgery. A legend indeed.

Oxshott Village Sports Club
Thank you. For being my 12-hour-a-week tennis companions for so many years. For inviting me to so many occasions after I got ill and never forgetting about me. You sent flowers and never stopped calling. In all sincerity, I am determined to be back, passing you all down the line, closing you down at the net in doubles and maybe even enjoying a Pimms or two on Finals Day.

Friends and Family International
Thank you. To so many wonderful friends and family that sent love far and wide. You will never know the impact you had at my weakest moments. For the hundreds of messages, phone calls and visits of love, I'm full of gratitude.

Austin Macauley, my publishers.
Thank you. You caught my attention because you strive to rise above. I didn't need a literary agent, a huge Instagram following or fame, because you took the bold step of reading the writing. You chose the message. A deep, heartfelt note of gratitude.

Thursday, February 8, 2018 – A Discovery

It's cold. We've hit -2 today. There's a sheen of glistening ice across the clay tennis court that makes the prerequisite sliding that much more dubious. My doubles partner marvels at how accurately I'm hitting the ball – with a certain fervour. Life is normal. A normal kind of good. The good that makes you assume. There lies an assumption of a happy family with a loving husband, two sons, a comfortable home and a fit, healthy body. It's one assumption too many.

Between noon and 4 pm that day, what is an irritating lump in my breast (that we have denounced as a cyst) is diagnosed as certifiable breast cancer. It's hard to blame the tools when you've had a mammogram, an ultrasound and multiple biopsies. I've travelled from a decent few sets of club tennis to breast cancer in one day, like light years in a time machine.

I have no emotions today. Although I can't look at my husband, his eyes tell the whole story. From the terror to the shock, to the fear of the unknown. To look and know that I'm the reason is the heaviest burden to carry. It's heavier than the cancer.

So far, we've been lulled into a diagnostic surgeon's management process of our emotions. It's going to be fine. 'A journey,' he says. One that likely involves "just" a lumpectomy, targeted chemotherapy, no mastectomy and unlikely hair loss. He is, after all, a specialist in aesthetics. This suddenly sounds fine to me. We've moved on from tennis. We're now on to the degrees of cancer. This sounds like the most palatable scenario, so I look at my husband and smile.

Jonathan

We've been together 19 years this year, married for 17. Enough to know that we've met our respective matches. Enough to realise that life without each other would be meaningless. I find emotion hard to come by; he finds it hard to park. His mission is to get me well again, mine is to make him laugh. I would much rather be in my place than his. As crazy as that sounds, I would never have found the smiles or the humour if this were him. I'm on a totally different plane. He doesn't understand where my inappropriate jokes and innuendos come from. I accept his somewhat unorthodox nickname for me – 'Bat Shit Crazy'.

Thursday, February 15, 2018 – The Diagnosis

An MRI and several biopsies later, my breast throbs and resembles the face of a downed boxer. And then it appears. The British answer to everything. Delivered by a smiling nurse, tray in hand, here comes the quintessential cup of tea. This symbol of hope, comfort and all things soluble. I'm not a betting woman, but I'm looking at this tea with an abundance of optimism.

The grimaces on Mr Diagnostic Surgeon's face should give it away but don't. We are blissfully in denial that diagnoses can be made without test results. Only those just came in. It was that scenario he didn't draw in his stickmen diagrams last week. That one called 'triple negative breast cancer' with likely full on chemo, radiotherapy followed by a mastectomy and definitely not much hair in sight. My husband is visibly shaking and I jokingly ask if I should order my funeral flowers. I'm told not just yet.

Friday, February 16, 2018 – Is There Secondary Cancer?

I coin it a "fab day out in London", otherwise known as a PET scan to ensure that all the Rosé in the Med hasn't caught up with me and transpired as deadly cancer elsewhere in the body. It's an "all body cancer and other crappy stuff" check. One negative tick. I'm positively excited. My husband treats me to expensive sushi, which takes me back to my childhood days in the Middle East when Mum used to take me to the bakery after the inevitable jab every time I got ill. It still feels good. I go into a mild panic about how I will look when visitors come over. I have visions of myself wafting about in kaftans and silk headscarves, martini in hand which quickly morphs into my current bobbly nighties, a head that resembles something out of a Star Trek movie and a Fortisip drink. Enter the fancy ostrich feather pyjamas. He picks them out, I think they are ridiculous, but my penchant for feathers mean they have to be bought – because they would make Joan Collins proud.

Our Boys

The boys took the news as most teenagers would. With some shock, upset and then a stoic return to teendom. This is the best place for them. As their mother, I want nothing more than their distraction from my disease and evolving condition. A school trip to California and a ski trip with their other Aunt cannot be timed well enough for the coming Easter break. Yet, I talk openly, answer questions and tell them there are no taboos. Secretly, I think my 15-year-old will think it quite cool when I announce my "Grade 1" shave all over. Please let this be the silver lining of losing one's hair. The younger of the two seems to find eternal bliss on his Xbox and in denial. I welcome this with open arms. Denial can sometimes be the key tool for survival. Whenever I need comfort, I turn to my bedside and look at their smiling faces. Our common denominator is the smile.

Sunday, February 18, 2018 – Mum

It's a date worth noting if Mum is here other than her one month in the summer for her pleasure trip. This is anything but. She has flown in from the States to be with me. Her face full of fortitude hides her heart full of fear. I find comfort all the same, just like I always have. My similar mission is to make her laugh, lighten her heart and feel okay. I think she expects me to cry but tears are nowhere in sight.

She fills our home as though she has always been there. All three of my boys share my comfort when she is around.

There is warmth, plenty of lovingly cooked food and conversation that stimulates the heart and mind. It's instant comfort for our family at a time when we need it the most.

Tuesday, February 20, 2018 – Finding Deeper Meaning

A meeting in a supposedly fabulous wig establishment. Oversized, overpriced wig fitted, check. Two-week delivery time and restyling, check. Date with a breast surgeon at leading hospital, check. It's here, in passing conversation, that brings me to this blog's raison d'être.

As I get changed, I overhear the light banter between my husband and the surgeon about how it's rare for Asians to get breast cancer. She insists it isn't. We won't investigate this very point until much later, but I had no idea at the time how poignant this conversation will become.

A Qualified Sister-In-Law

There are times when you get just plain lucky. My husband's sister has not only practised as an oncologist but has a PhD in cancer research. That, and she cares because she's family. Jonathan spends hours with her on the phone, furiously scribbling notes and posing questions. It helps to feel somewhat in control, and by getting me the best treatment and in the best hands, this is, mission accomplished. She quickly hones down the best surgeon and oncologist for the job. Referrals are sent so he is quick to secure them. She is constantly checking on my every detail via text and phone. We as a family, are very lucky to have her.

Tuesday, March 6, 2018 – EC Chemotherapy Cycle 1

It's my first day of "EC" chemo. Apparently, the harsh one. I've had a port installed in my chest (day surgery the week prior). The plan is four three weekly cycles. As Mum and Jonathan sit by me, I grit through the application of the cold cap. The nurse walks away as I marvel at how easy this cold cap business is. It's actually not that cold at all. What a big to-do over nothing. I learn, upon the return of the nurse, that she has forgotten to switch it on…okay, so now it's cold. Migraine cold. Arctic on my head with a roll and ice cream on top cold. My hair had better be worth this as it gives the phrase "brain freeze" new meaning. After pre-meds, I'm ready for the red stuff. Two big injections go into my port. Then a clear one. I'm wondering whether I'm feeling light hearted or headed as I doze off. I realise the irony that the cancer is not yet going to make me feel ill, it's the chemo that will. But what's poison for the body is also poison for the cancer. It's time for the body to take a hit for the team.

My Best Friend

My best friend of 31 years passed away just shy of three months ago. I haven't stopped grieving and perhaps never will. It accounts for one of the worst days of my life. But now, she whispers to me all the time. I hear her voice cheering me on, giving me strength, and most importantly being that shining example of the greatest kind of bravery. She battled with illness for years and protected me from the worst of it while she fought hard. Now she breathes new life into me every day. She is my whispering angel.

Saturday, March 10, 2018 – Unusual Reactions

It's 6 am and my joints are in so much pain, I can't stand. To say my stomach is delicate sounds a bit too poetic. To say it's like a scene from 'Bridesmaids' is probably more accurate. I have my first sense of humour failure when my husband asks whether I'm okay. The hospital visit, which is supposed to be a friendly check on said symptoms, turns into a five-day stay. Five days where I learn that hospitals on weekends might as well pose as a morgue and therefore, in my furtive imagination have turned into a monument for the devil incarnate. I've had severe *'neutropenia'*. Essentially, despite an injection to ensure my white blood cells (which are responsible for immunity) are kept high, they surge and then plummet to below 0.5, making me massively vulnerable to infection. The Prof has been on a conference abroad but returns fully briefed to the minute. On day five, my sense of humour has kicked back in with my health and I announce that unless he discharges me, I intend to leap out of the first story window like a superhero from hell. He smiles wondering if I'm half-serious and says it will be fine for me to take the lobby.

A Core Support System

It's been said many a time, but these are the moments in life when you find out who your people are. I've been overwhelmed by support. From childhood friends texting almost daily to school mums forming a group WhatsApp to check on me while others send gifts from the Year group. International messages of support have come from friends and family far and wide in our global village. Flowers cover my fireplace hearth which bely many "just gave birth" jokes but indicate how many have been so thoughtful. Visits from my tennis club friends and then just a handful of family doing what only a family can do. To say this is normal is to diminish the effect people can ultimately have. Their support is actually life-altering and I will be forever grateful.

Thursday, March 15, 2018 – Hospital Round 1: Over

I have never slept in the day, and I have never watched daytime TV. During my time in the hospital, Mum and I have become strangely quizzical about and bemused by *'Four in a Bed'*, which despite its title surprisingly lives up to its daytime slot. Couples of B&B contestants battle it out to be paid the highest value for money in one jazzy little programme. Who knew? I draw the line at *'A Place in the Sun'*, but have developed an odd affection for the narrator of *'Come Dine with Me'*. Dave Lamb is a newfound legend.

In the cab on the way home with my Mum, the thing I delight in first is greenery. I haven't seen the ground floor of planet Earth in five days. A leaf, a blade of grass, and the abundance of trees literally feed the endorphins that release instantly. When you go through these tunnels, it's not just the humour but indeed greenery that brings figurative and literal calm. Home has never smelt so good. My beautiful Ragdoll hasn't looked this grateful to see me in her little life.

Rani the Ragdoll

She came into our home a tiny Ragdoll at eight weeks old in October 2015. In true Ragdoll fashion, she would collapse in our arms to sleep, cry like a baby if she needed attention and run to greet us when we walked in the door. We were all left completely smitten. Less a cat more a playful, loving puppy, we appropriately named her Rani or 'Queen' in Hindi. She has lived up to her name. She is the Queen of our hearts and since I have become unwell, I can see the love I have poured into her. She follows me around tentatively after my chemo when I walked way too slow for her recognition. She waits patiently outside my bathroom door if I disappear for too long. She can do a worried expression better than an artist from the Royal Shakespeare Company. She sleeps by my feet during the day, a time she knows I have never slept.

Sunday, March 18, 2018 – Hospital Calling

My euphoric appreciation for all things "home" has come to an end like a rude awakening. My fever is rising above the chemo emergency card levels. I try and convince my husband that he's bought a faulty thermometer. When all else fails, blame your tools. He's not buying it and apologetically picks up the phone to call the emergency number. Hospital calling again. This is probably the closest tears have come (they would rush back down if they had known what was coming). By the time I have my coat on, I can barely stand and I start to shake wondering if I've been stripped naked on the North Pole. Rani watches me with a perfected Oscar-worthy worried look. I find myself offering her words of comfort and tell her I'll be home soon. A white lie, I'm secretly telling myself.

'Spectacular Sepsis'

I have borrowed this phrase from the Prof and I would describe it as a force personified. It's like a proverbial monster that has come to life in my body, terrorising my family, whilst panicking the most seasoned team of doctors. For five days, I have rigours (similar to never-ending convulsions or shakes whereby it feels like you're running a marathon that your body can't run, but can't stop). This is followed by a disappointingly consistent 104-degree fever which eventually puts you to sleep with help from an IV paracetamol. The IV medication can only give relief every six hours to protect the liver. The rigours and fever are spiking every four hours.

Two days and my blood tests show nothing. Though my breast is in agony, burning and red. Problem number two. A radiologist confirms cellulitis, an inflammatory infection caused by one of my biopsies. Like some cataclysm my blood tests come back, this time showing sepsis. An infection in the blood that they tell me is up to a marker of 446. When I ask what the baseline or normal reading is, they say 'zero'. This is enough to start me on a "Domestos" dose of three different antibiotics.

Tuesday, March 20, 2018 – Unresponsive

Like some joke spiralled out of control, I am not responding to this particular cocktail of antibiotics. Pain, fevers and shakes become a daily marathon. I am now monitored with observations on the hour, through the night. Prolonged sleep becomes a distant memory. Blood test syringes early mornings in my arm jolt me awake. They change my antibiotics once again.

I have a slew of visitors the following day. In a bizarre way, I'm trying to talk and laugh at their jokes through my rigours. My uncle keeps rabbiting on about some friend of his that is settling in England. He makes jokes while I shake uncontrollably, forcing my ever-ready smile. There is discomfort when I stop responding and perhaps relief when I fall asleep. I'm still hoping they've had enough positive feedback.

Where problems have solutions, those solutions, in turn, cause further problems. I develop tachycardia and hypotension. To you and I that is a fast heartbeat at rest and low blood pressure. My diastolic rate has drops to 83, which results in the fast pumping of IV fluids to raise my blood pressure back up. These fluids are administered fast and often. The blood pressure and heart rate are evidently a further complication.

As my blood pressure starts to rise, another issue rears its ugly head. My blood vessels have leaked fluid out into other parts of my body causing seven extra kilos of fluid to swell my legs, stomach, arms and face. I could easily be advertising Michelin tyres or stars. Not sure which. Breathing is difficult as my lungs have filled up with fluid at the bottom. I go into mild panic as I think of M. She passed from lung disease and I try to imagine this, her daily predicament. She talks me through each breath that does not come easily.

As they wheel me into a CT scan, I can feel my head swaying from side to side from the cocktail of drugs that would bemuse most pharmacists. With my enlarged limbs boasting lots of IV fluid, sore eyes are what I'm a sight for. Time to have a laugh, life says. A bouncy, jovial nurse thrusts a form under my face to 'help me focus'. We stumble through the questions pausing slightly on the final one. As though I've just auditioned for a smoking '50 shades' sequel, she earnestly asks if there is any chance, I could be pregnant. Incredulously, I look at her and reply, 'Not unless my name's Mary, love.'

There is a point in all of this whereby the severity of my sepsis is coming to a fever pitch. There are seven physicians in my room and there is talk of potential blood transfusions and transferring me to the high dependency unit in Chelsea. Apparently, the cancer right now is the least of my problems. Like an informative teleprompter, I just have to look at my husband's face to read between the lines.

Friday, March 23, 2018 – Catheters and Hair Loss

My survival instinct has kicked in as I start to react to the new antibiotics. The fever is reluctant but starts to come down from 40.1, for what seems like an eternity, to 39.5 marking its gradual descent. Finally, I stop shaking. What is reality for physicians and loved ones is very different for a patient in and out of the capacity to think straight. When the word 'catheter' is mentioned as a method of draining all my fluids, it is the trigger that unleashes my inner hysteria. I beg my husband to refuse on my behalf as if it's a sentence worse than death. He looks at me and tells me to stay calm and do what needs to be done. I won't dwell on the next four days.

To add insult to injury, my hair is threatening an Asian impersonation of Donald Trump's comb over. Don't want to get controversial here but it's not a look I've ever aspired to. It falls in clumps every time I run my hands or a brush through it. I am amused by the times I have cursed how much hair I have had in the past I fill up three tall hospital bins and yet it keeps coming. I hear M again saying it's just hair, that I need to just get on with it. With her, I always did what I was told, so straight talk works like a charm. I later learn from the Prof that even without the chemo, with this level of sepsis, my hair never stood a chance.

Though one thing I receive does unlock some emotion. I am sent a necklace that M used to love and wore often. It is a beautiful long chain adorned with rubies and jade on a shimmery gold string. I imagine it on her, a tall, slender picture of elegance and the vision is so vivid it warms me. For a few moments, I let my tears come, for her at least and promise myself to wear it on my birthday.

Monday, March 26, 2018 – My 47th birthday

My swelling has gone down and I'm able to consider a shower. After much pleading, my catheter is out and it is the biggest birthday present I have ever received. My mum spends every day in the hospital with me, my husband, every evening. Today he will come early to try and emulate our annual celebrations. These are not shoes, you or I would care to fill. And yet he does it all with a smile.

I'm sitting with my mum when out of nowhere, the entire ward's nurses burst in with a birthday serenade sporting a beautiful, exotic cake that looks like it was baked in Antigua this morning. I am so touched by their kindness and reflect on how many people have dedicated their time to look after me, nursing me back to some semblance of health and yet with more cheery smiles along the way.

At 4 pm, my husband walks in with gifts, cards, cake, non-alcoholic wine and emoji balloons to boot. It's one of those times in life that renders one speechless. That someone can love another quite so much. I read all the beautiful cards from friends and family. There are phone calls, texts, gifts and glamorous footwear that would make the 'A list' gasp. My sons have sent presents and cards so carefully thought about, so opulent, should I not feel spoilt on my day. I marvel at how blessed I feel even in my current predicament. Who couldn't be happy today?

Finally, I am stabilised. The cellulitis is subsiding albeit the slowest to respond while the sepsis marker is down to 37. I can now appreciate that I have stayed alive (which apparently was in question at one point in the last two weeks). This neatly segues into the gargantuan dilemma of chemo and shrinking the two breast lumps and two lymph nodes that are fertile with cancer.

Going home is the boon I've been dreaming of. Seeing Rani skip and prance around excitedly is the icing on the cake. Delicious smells come from the kitchen where my mum labours over the stove as she has been doing daily despite her 75 years and counting. Being home is the best elixir though I quickly turn my mind back to one stark reality – the very first step of treating my cancer has gone horribly wrong.

Thursday, April 5, 2018 – New Chemo Regime

The Prof declares EC chemo too dangerous for me now. We are on Plan B. Plan B was supposed to occur after Plan A which I can no longer complete. I wonder whether this has compromised my treatment. I'm told that it has not, but that the cycle of this next treatment is going to be longer, less harsh but now it's weekly.

It's the first day of my Taxol chemo together with a drug called Carboplatin. More new substances and more of the unknown. Mum is busy chatting to our chemo neighbours on the ward sharing stories of inappropriate accessory pairings in this month's Elle. I'm getting drowsier by the minute with the plethora of pre-meds which include what feels like a ton of anti-histamines, steroids and anti-sickness IVs through my port. Here comes the Taxol. Just 10 ml in, my discomfort begins. I start to feel my airways constrict. There is heat rising through my head and all does not feel well. I call the nurse who cannot disconnect me fast enough. After a consultation with doctors, I'm administered more pre-meds, given an hour's interval and can finally tolerate the Taxol this time. Is it onwards and upwards they say?

My Sister the Photographer

My sister and I have always had a very consistent relationship. As you go through life, this is something you come to value. I think my cancer has hit her quite hard. No one has quite had the mindset that this could ever possibly happen to me, especially not Sadia. She has been very supportive and now a different type of support kicks in. We talk about my blog, about its mission and how we can potentially harness something inherently negative into something positive. As a budding photographer, what Sadia finds instinctive is capturing the mood, electricity and emotions of her subjects. Just 10 days after my sepsis, on one of my few "good" days, she arranges a shoot. Sadia calls our friend Debbie Storey (a renown make-up artist already championing this cause) who offers to come and do my makeup while she and her husband, Ian creatively prep for the photography. The results are as authentic as I imagined.

Saturday, April 7, 2018 – A Photo Shoot

I've slowly gathered strength, built up my diet and started to gain back some weight. Energy is slowly seeping back into my body – just enough anyway. I have to get rid of what is left of my hair first. I'm not relishing the thought, but equally, have little left to be proud of.

I text one of the lovely girls from my local salon that I've gone to for years and they send Hannah. Sweet, sensitive, calm and "done it all before", is exactly what I need. She immediately puts me at ease. I am browsing through a magazine featuring models that have their heads shaved declaring great empowerment. All I can say is, it's more empowering when you have a choice.

I can hear the whirring of the razor as its cold blade glides effortlessly across my head. I can see what is left of the shorter bob I have cut fall to the floor. Its fall from grace is still quite alarming and surprisingly profuse. Frankenstein is not a look I'm in favour of. GI Jane is definitely taking over this scene.

She says I can go and have a look in the mirror. Reluctantly, I walk over. It's weirdly what I expected, yet no prettier than I'd imagined. Still, this is yet another milestone of acceptance that I have to go through and smile through it I will. I can't quite let anyone but my photographic entourage see it. I'm not feeling that brave. The irony of where these photographs will end up is not lost on me.

Thursday, April 12, 2018 – Week 2 of Plan B Chemo

My sister is with me today. I'm documenting this session, talking optimistically into her camera about how I need to tolerate this chemo else the future is well, unknown.

Pre-meds again and with some trepidation, I watch as they plug the Taxol in. Just three ml this time, it feels much worse than last week. My airwaves constrict again but faster as my face goes crimson, coughing and spluttering, I reach for my panic button wondering if the nurse will make it from the other side of the room in time. Nurses and a doctor rush in, the partition curtains pulled shut much to the bemused curiosity of the other patients and my sister is left holding the phone a little frozen from what I can see. The chemo is stopped and I can breathe again but clearly, my body has pre-empted quite a staunch dislike to my new regime.

The Prof is not far behind this incident. The look on his face is saying I cannot be serious with the intensity of John McEnroe. Amused, I grin cheekily and ask him if perhaps he might want to get some pointe shoes, as I clearly like to keep people on their toes. Deep down, I'm wondering what Plan C is.

Plan C is a new drug again. This one is called Abraxane and unlike Taxol, it carries the same drug but it is bound by albumin as opposed to the protein binding in Taxol that my body has vehemently rejected. It's mainly approved for metastatic and pancreatic cancers. So again, from what I understand, a slightly unprecedented territory is being explored. I am the eternal optimist.

To add to my confidence, my little brother flies in from the States for the weekend. I'm not able to join a fun trip to the pub for lunch but home is full of food, love and good chats. As my brother flies home, I feel sad to see him go but grateful for the positive energy he has left behind with me.

Thursday, April 19, 2018 – Plan C Chemo

I arrive like the unsuspecting experiment awaiting yet another trial with Mum in tow, furrowed brows and all. They start with the Carboplatin, my new tried and tested friend. Pre-meds again and I find myself silently praying that my reaction is to protein vs. albumin. As the chemo seeps comfortably through my veins, my heartbeat returns to a comfortable seated trot rather than a frenetic canter. I have tolerated Plan C. We are on a roll forward for the first time.

Relieved beyond comprehension, Mum and I start to walk out and I bump into one of the doctors I remember from the sepsis days. She asks how I am and when I tell her I've just tolerated my first chemo, she nods, fully informed and says she's been reading my files. Not the kind of celebrity I'd hoped to be as a child, but I'll take it. Two sessions and two weeks pass without incident.

Thursday, May 3, 2018 – Inspiration from Elsewhere

This week I walk confidently into the chemo ward like it's my new home away from home. The nurses chat happily and other patients become familiar faces to wave and say hello to.

I suddenly get the social attraction of Bingo, well, just for a second anyway.

They say a potentially terminal illness is a great leveller. It doesn't matter whether you live in a remote village in Asia or in England's pastures green the fight for life is allegedly the same. But today, a lady I've seen a couple of times strikes up a conversation that moves me to the core yet again. She's smiling, very chatty and looks like she has tonnes of energy. As her story unfolds, I find myself struggling to comprehend. Her condition is incurable and inoperable. She is having chemo to prolong her life and to try and shrink secondary cancer.

Her husband walks in, another upbeat figure. His eyes show a vulnerability though and now I understand why. They are taking life in three-month chunks which concluded last week with a scan that revealed her cancer has not spread but has not shrunk either. So here they are again, starting another round of chemo as a stab at another chance.

Their story is beyond moving as I am struck by the power of their dual force. I find myself telling stories about how special moments have been created at home, just because of the cancer. Perhaps events that would never have taken place. Relationships have strengthened, unsaid feelings vocalised and laughter has filled our home for the most insane reasons. We must spend our time creating these moments. That is all I can say to this amazing couple whose relationship speaks volumes and optimism knows no bounds. I leave humbled and inspired.

Thursday, May 10, 2018 – This Is About You.
LEARN

I decide to go to chemo on my own today. A kind of rite of passage. Good to say I can, and yes, I've managed to survive it emotionally as well. These things in life can at times be as large or as small as you make them. It is a very large deal when someone takes the time to accompany me to chemo. It's a relatively small one when I choose to go alone.

So this one's about you. As I reflect on last week and continue to be amazed at how individual everyone's journey is, one thread runs across it all. Everyone's journey is unique, so know your body. I know some people who will sit months with alleged niggles that were ultimately serious and others who will consider an MRI the holy grail for a sore throat. There's a balance to be had but balance is key.

Your body is a person that will talk. It will tell you when things aren't running smoothly, it will also be a moany cow for nothing but it will shout when it's very unhappy because something is going horribly wrong. My layman's advice is this: Listen. Evaluate. Alert. Respond. Notify.

LEARN.

Listen – If you have a physical sign, or an unexplained pain, hear it.

Evaluate – Does this occur often, is it changing your life in any way, is it a known tell-tale sign?

Alert – tell someone who cares about you more than you. Pester power is the best.

Respond – If they're nagging you and you're nagging you, it's probably time for action.

30

Notify – Let your physician know. Respect their expertise from here on.

Thursday, May 17, 2018 – The Power of Positivity: A World of Clichés

It's chemo solo again this week. I am mindful that I have just two weeks to go before my scan. The ultrasound that will tell me what my cancer's been up to while it's been treated with chemotherapy. Is it playing with me? Is it simply resistant and here to stay, or is it picking up sticks and running for the hills, lymph nodes and all. An emotional maze lies ahead to navigate.

I feel immediately stupid when I say to the nurse, 'I try to stay positive.' I liken it to one of those moments in an interview when I used to ask about someone's best qualities and out came 'I'm a people person.' In a service industry, that has to be categorically the worst reply in interviewer world. Or the other one, where you ask where someone's biggest weakness lies and their comeback is 'I'm a perfectionist'. Cringe.

And cringe I do at my own cliché. But when the nurse looks back at me, she says, 'You'll be surprised. This doesn't work so well with the negative ones.' My clichéd, very uncool (or as my sons would say in street speak, 'unsafe') soul feels a bit better. As I bounce home on steroids and other meds, my optimism takes a bit of a bashing this week and the next. Despite telling the doctors I'm doing really well and pretending I could take part in the Olympics; the cumulative effects of the chemo are definitely rearing their heads. A little more fatigue, joint pain, more hair loss (it had started to grow back for a while) and lots of nausea. But I still consider myself fortunate compared to some of the effects chemo can cause. I marvel daily at the spectrum of people that suffer harsher chemo regimes with far greater side effects. I'm going to keep marching and feeling grateful for the little things.

Thursday, May 3, 2018 – My First Ultrasound since Chemotherapy

We don't sleep very well that Wednesday night. I always arm myself with the worst-case scenario, just so the expression on my face doesn't change if they say, 'There has been no change' or 'It has spread despite the chemo.' Jonathan and I sit in the car, eerily silent, but I know he is cautiously optimistic. First stop, bloods. These are checked by a doctor (a two-hour process before my chemo can be confirmed). As my husband sits flinching when they are taking blood, quite painlessly, I find myself giggling at his reaction. The other patients start to smile as he darts about the chemo ward pretending to admire the car park scenery.

Next, the ultrasound. I find myself clutching M's necklace for comfort. She's always with me but so much more so on these occasions. I establish a good banter with the radiologist as we chat about chemo ports, inventions and the med. I don't expect him to reveal anything when he asks how I feel about any changes in my body. I say I feel positive. That the larger lump I first discovered doesn't feel so large anymore. To my huge relief, still guiding the ultrasound, he concurs I'm correct. The cancer has definitely shrunk, though an MRI is needed to determine how much. The lymph nodes are still showing cells but are on the 'upper end of normal'. The chemotherapy is working and I for one am elated. Another round of chemo and we drive home with great relief in our hearts. The best part of my day? Delivering good news to all my friends and family for a change. I will be delivering smiles again.

Sunday, June 3, 2018 – A Topsy-Turvy Anniversary

It's our 17th wedding anniversary to the day. We've been together 19 years and we've celebrated ever since. This year we've decided we're not going to do just the two of us. The boys have been working hard for exams over half term and as it comes to a close, we are going to go in to London as a foursome to their favourite sushi restaurant. I will suffer the excruciating pain of not being able to eat the Hamachi with jalapeno as all things raw are off the menu for me, lest I want infection. A lovely lunch is had, a few treats, shopping for us all and we return home feeling satiated and undeniably normal. I remember so often M used to say, 'there's a whole world out there'. I now know how cheered up she felt to step back into it once in a while, like nothing was happening in the background. I feel her joy.

In my elation, I've forgotten to give myself the injection that boosts my white blood cells, so it's the first port of call when I get home. These injections are a boost to the immune system but as they stimulate bone marrow, they cause flu-like symptoms and joint pain. I inject these two days a week.

My joy is short lived. Having also taken my steroid medication too late (clearly distracted by the lack of permission to consume raw fish), I can't sleep. So I'm still pounding away at my keyboard responding to a friend at midnight when all of a sudden I feel the strangest chest pain and a tightening of my throat. 'Ignore this, it will pass', I keep telling myself. But my breathing becomes more difficult and the pain starts to radiate to the same place in my upper back. I start pacing thinking walking will help. I sip water hoping my paracetamol has stupidly gotten stuck in my oesophagus. Nothing is settling my chest. Twenty minutes go by and the pain is getting more intense. I must admit this is the one time I'm thinking, *Just my bloody luck. It'll be a heart attack or aneurysm that will kill me and there will be no dramatic goodbyes in sight.*

Monday, June 4, 2018 – A Night in A&E

It takes me a while to think about waking Jonathan. He usually has all the answers. He will not only tell me what to do, but it will go the minute he opens his eyes. The only look I get is a wide-eyed stare at 1 am when I know he's thinking 'So my daily alarm at 4:30 am should be fun today'. We run through a few scenarios and he gets on Google. Deep joy. Google, never an optimistic story told. The panic is rising in me a bit as is the pain. There is no position that makes it subside.

Finally, he reaches for our yellow emergency card number. To my utter horror, the first announcement on the automated message says 'If you are experiencing chest pain, call 999. Bugger. As the operator goes through her litany of questions, it becomes obvious that something could be very wrong here and I can't go unchecked. Double bugger. She asks about any previous heart attacks, blood clots, aneurysms and the list is long. She concludes that an ambulance is on its way.

Two of the loveliest ladies appear in our driveway armed with an ECG monitor and all the kind words one can muster at 1:30 am. They are simply missing a halo in my book as they help make up the world's unsung heroes. My charts look just about okay apart from a double peak in heart rate that she says forces her to recommend that I go to A&E and get a blood test to confirm there has been no cardiac incident.

As Jonathan briefs our sleeping son and follows me in his car, I chat to the medic in the ambulance as I start to feel the pain subside. Typical, I think. Probably was just a crazy paracetamol stuck in my passageways. I check this with her and she says the timings don't make sense for that scenario as it would have long dissolved with the water and time.

A&E is full. I'm wheeled in amongst corridors of people lying listlessly after their Sunday nights have gone seriously pear-shaped. Eventually, they find me a cubicle at 2 am and proceed to do more ECG and blood tests. The nurse hacks my veins to pieces in three places to get a cannula in (apparently my veins are too 'delicate') and eventually gives up to a male nurse who stops the carnage. That chick really needs to go back to vein-finding finishing school.

I'm now playing the waiting game and listening to my "competition". The question that begs all night is why? Why are they doing this to their lives? Here I am fighting to stay alive and there they are playing with their mortality as if it has no meaning. There's two policemen babysitting the guy who has been on a bender of drugs and alcohol, harassing his father for money and then been reported missing. Then next door is the guy, who's washed down a whole bottle of paracetamol with a bottle of vodka, thankfully threw it up and stayed alive. Then, the poor 88-year-old lady who lies alone smiling opposite me with a fractured spine. I find this so much more distressing than anything I'm going through. I'm not good with human suffering and I'm lying at the epicentre of it.

We finally get to see a doctor at 7:30 am. Short of begging, I'm in a desperate, pleading position to get discharged and promise to take up the issue with my oncologist. After a clear chest X-ray and some questions about my blood test, I see daylight again. There is a spring in my step just to expedite my journey out of the hell I've just witnessed. A&E on a Sunday night is the one thing that could put most diehard optimists to bed for good. It hasn't conquered this one though.

Thursday, June 7, 2018 – Sweet Chemo and Cola Bottles

I have willed myself to hate sugar since the 'ballet days'. Chocolate, sweets, cakes, puddings, hell even sorbet are sparingly "tasted" a few times a year. I am in denial about their true divinity. This can only be a good thing, until now. Can someone tell me what it is about the concoction of pre-meds or chemo that causes a sugar averse, dieter to morph into a chipmunk storing Haribos? I've turned into a saliva-wielding maniac with severely animated pouches, sorry cheeks? My sister took one look at me last week and bursts into giggles wondering where the serial cola bottle killer in her car has come from. This week, my husband watches me plough into a chocolate Magnum with such fervour he thinks

I might snatch his wedding ring and thread it onto the splintered stick as my newfound partner in life.

Thankfully, after a day or so, I turn back into the gentle, 'no thank you, it's not for me' polite, sugar refrainer. I only realise now, how irritating I must be. Sorry but that's the way it's going to be. And for all you ardent food critics, I am well aware of the theory that sugar is bad for cancer. That is as irritating as my aversion of it! For all others, if you want a sugar fest riot with a sweet junkie, please join me on Sweet Chemo Thursdays. The steroids make me a tad edgy too. You shall not be disappointed on the entertainment front.

On the news side, it's pretty good. The Prof is delighted with my ultrasound and all the shrinkage it alludes to. Next step is to talk with my breast surgeon. The cancer is working and an MRI can be in a few weeks' time but chemo needs to go the course. My surgery timing will depend on three things; my tolerance of the chemo and quality of life, the tingling in my fingers and toes (which though sounds like some minor pins and needles, is actually long-term nerve damage) and my blood work (not showing lowered immunity). So here comes stage two. Those conversations. That surgery. My body.

Sunday, June 17, 2018 – High Tea, Hibernation and a Chemo Offload

My son has finished his Common Entrance exams and is off on his Leavers trip for a week. We have planned an escape. An escape from the reality that has plagued us for the last few months, a gentle reminder (as M used to say) of the fact that 'there is a whole world out there'.

As I pack my cocktail of required medications, make endless lists for Rani's caretaker about safety precautions that would make most health and safety institutions baulk, I realise I'm clinging on to where I have been hiding. As open as one thinks they may be about any one situation, it is always alarming when you catch yourself out doing the very thing you vowed you would never do. In my case, hide.

An hour late (I'm never late), I'm successfully extracted from all things familiar in a venture to the New Forest. As the manmade motorways start to peel away, I'm enchanted by the green, open vistas (vistas are my new thing) that lead up to this beautiful house/hotel where we are staying. What surprises me is how much I love the anonymity. No one notices my hair is not my own, no one looks at me with cancerous pity and for a little bit, no one thinks or knows any truth about me.

But then the guilt of not completing my blog, not posting on social media, dropping my cause in any way does begin to haunt me. Haunting subjects make you think. A thinker I will always be. It's here that I will venture into a very controversial topic that frankly is driving me insane. The number of healthy, yoga busting, fit as fiddle people that tell me chemotherapy is a 'scam'.

People. First, it's probably prudent to have a little hop, skip or a tiny jump in someone's shoes before you detail what choices you would make in their situation. Second, let's talk about odds here. I find it unbelievably irresponsible of journalists to showcase one person on a morning show that has been miraculously cured by cannabis oil and the like when there are millions that have responded to proper cancer treatment.

In my thinker's head, there are select things that have struck me about people's response to chemotherapy, including my own. One, the fear of pain and the change of one's appearance. Two, fear of failure. Three, a deep-seated suspicion of corporate greed and corruption. Last, the belief of and faith in the media glorifying singular success stories of alternative therapies.

I have felt all of these fears, but when you are staring at your two young sons and husband, you see their desperation for you to be well. Or if you look at your parent who cannot abide the thought of walking the earth a day without you, when you look at your life and think, this is not my time – I for one, am not going to say 'no problem, I'll go and smoke a few doobies.'

Homoeopathic remedies are great. Positive eating is brilliant. Cut out all the toxins. You now have an empowered immune system. This is the best start possible if you're going to fight a disease of any kind. But please find me the person that will tell you, with statistical confidence (sorry but when your life flashes before you, I dare you not to play the numbers game), that there is high precedence of treating your cancer and making it retreat through natural remedies or Ayurveda. I'm going with statistical confidence all the way. I need it, I demand it. I will bow to it every time. Now, where's that high tea?

Tuesday, June 26, 2018 – Shopping and Surgery

Today is just supposed to be another day. Another appointment. Another benign (no pun intended) conversation.

I'm going in to London, guising my situation with escape, shopping and all things frivolous. I know it is anything but. This week, the GI situation has imploded a bit so very weak from it all, feeling a bit dizzy, I pretend it's just a usual jaunt for me. Footloose and fancy-free. Though I'm stumbling and this is not the hippy shopping chick I recognise. I also can't see anything. Shopping racks appear to be standing in a haze of white. Yesterday, I had decided to go to a different branch of my supermarket where the car park was at an incline. Imagine my surprise when I went flying downhill into a busy road lead by crazy supermarket trolley until a young lad stopped it and guided me back to my car. I was so frustrated by this OAP scenario, I thanked him and scurried along like some old lady I already loathe. Who the hell is this person?

I leave myself two hours before my appointment as I don't think I can walk for much more. It's a scalding 30 degrees centigrade and London is at its finest. I'll admit it, I'm temporarily lulled. Lulled by London, lulled by denial and happy about it to boot. I've done a bit of research. Skin sparing mastectomies, blah blah blah.

But when I enter that office, a new reality hits. One I thought I'd done all my homework for. My surgeon is nothing short of not just being a genius but also having the experience, integrity and confidence. She could tell me I had five heads and I would just nod. This lady is just exemplary. She examines me and is so encouraged by the change of form that seems to be literally shedding the cancer. Her face is full of positivity.

Then we sit down to talk. What is an expected, routine conversation feels very unexpected Yet I don't understand why. I've spent hours scouring the internet, preparing, being in denial, taking piece by piece, doing just what they've told me to do and I'm still slightly shocked.

Surgery is in September. There is absolutely no argument for no surgery. Surgery does not spread the cancer that does not already want to spread. Surgery is absolutely necessary to preserve my chances at life.

The next sentence is something I will remember for the rest of my days. 'Right now, the two most important conversations of your life ever, are the following; the day you got diagnosed and the day we do the surgery, examine the pathology and tell you what we found.' The pathology is my prognosis for life. It will give my surgeon an idea of what my cancer is about, what my odds are for it coming back and what chances I have at life. I had not expected that.

Her experience speaks volumes, she is compassionate and yet she is straight. I love that. It's what I can depend on, the truth. That's all anyone wants at any stage in life. You can live with the truth. She tells me I'm responding well to the chemo, that my tumour was large and invasive to start with, but we have good signs here. But here's the thing, no one can give me any guarantees.

So we have surgery, then reconstruction, then radiotherapy (another huge nod towards necessity) then a long road of being monitored, but fingers crossed the initial signs are good. I miss M so much right now. I swear if I could see her in that waiting room, I'd almost look forward to it. But she's not there and never will be, but she will always whisper in my ears no matter what. The silver lining after a conversation like that is my mum is on a flight back from the US to be with me. This is the most comforting thing I can think of right now. Mummy love right back at me. I've tried

41

with my boys, but I really need some of my own medicine right now. And at my age, to have that, I'm blessed. M would be the first person to tell me that.

Wednesday, 4 July, 2018 – Plastic Surgery and Kurran's Last Days at Prep School

This week is a marathon. It's Kurran's end of term Leavers week. Gulp. I have bloods and chemo confirmation today (which I've moved from Thursday) so that I can "nip" in tomorrow morning and have my chemo before his sports day and Leavers play. My plastic surgeon's office has called a meeting at 8 pm in London. That, has my head in a tail spin. My high fluting ideas of pointing and clicking at some glamorous reconstruction catalogue are well…flailing at best.

So off I trek to my nearer branch of said hospital. After giving bloods, I sit down with the doctor who has to ask how my neuropathy is handling the drugs and how I'm feeling in general. I'm very irritated that my muscles seem to be getting weaker and tiredness is on the rise. This is not someone I recognise, so I'm going at it full pelt regardless. He raises his eyebrows after I say I'm dropping my son home from school and driving in to London for a second appointment. At this point he tells me I'm in my fifth cycle of Carboplatin and asks whether I have any idea how heavy duty that chemo is. I look incredulous (denial has some kick ass expressions). No, I reply. He says this last month will be difficult and declining. If I'm to be honest, I take little heed as I do think going to bed with that statement makes for some seriously floppy muscles. Okay, revelation today. Tick. Will rest when I need to.

Next appointment is in London with an allegedly brilliant plastic surgeon who will work in tandem with my other surgeon, whom I trust impeccably. Okay, so he's good. Experienced, calming and honest as all hell. After a fairly good banter, he looks perplexed and tells me my case is 'complicated'. Not quite what I had expected. He very rationally highlights and sketches the reason for it. There is just the one reason. There is a full mastectomy slap bang in the middle of his mission to make me look as good as possible. The complications arise because every case and body is different. Mine's apparently too slim (doesn't hide a multitude of sins) and there is a question as to whether there is enough excess tissue in my tummy for this apparent tummy tuck, I'm supposed to have. Otherwise known as an ideal DIEP flap surgery which uses your body's natural tissue, blood vessels and skin. For someone who's always thought I was closer to a Teletubby than Rosie Huntington Whiteley, this is somewhat perplexing to me. My husband calls it body dysmorphia.

Then comes the bomb. He tells me that I'm young, I have a good slender figure, a good shape and really there is nothing wrong with the way that I present. This is news to me. He says he can't make me look as good as I do now. Err, pardon? This, in my head (thanks to last crazy plastic surgeon whom I no longer see), is not quite what I had in mind. This whole looking like a 20-year-old while it should all be going south, whilst bouncing around with a flat stomach on our boat in the med, now that was what I had in mind. I tell him, I like straight talk and I want to hear it like it is. He says not to leave despondent; he will do the best he can do and that it will be a year of procedures ensuring I have the best possible outcome.

OK. In the First World War, this code carried the meaning "zero killed". I hark back to this and consider that 'there were zero people killed in the relaying of this message.' This is my usual scraping the bottom of the positivity barrel. The crisp visions of flouncing around in flower-appliqued bikinis on beaches in Menorca with a full head of hair are blurring. Instead, I'm looking at the scar lines as he draws them on my imaginary previously unscarred body. Okay, I say, I'll add myself to that "scars are beautiful" Instagram campaign to raise awareness. What did my friend say on FB the other day? Scars make for beautiful stories. All true. For just an hour or so, a little sadness, a little grief for the old me sets in. Then, I take my new reality and start to spin the yarn in to new proverbial material again.

We arrive home. The boys are hovering and Mum is anxious to know the outcome of my meeting. Without hiding anything I start to relay an overall summary while sparing gory details for later. We all reach for just the one glass of Rosé. Meanwhile, my eldest boy has been sitting looking at his phone darting eyes back and forth into our conversation as we relish the transfer of conversation to first his teachers neatly segueing into history and barbaric leaders of the past. The Bay of Pigs, George Bush Sr., Stalin, General Mao, Hiroshima. I'm loving the intensity, the passion from all three of them. What a wonderful digression and end to my evening.

Thursday, 5 July, 2018 – Chemo, Sports Days and Leavers Plays

It has to be said, not feeling too bright today. Though my attitude is sky high. Mum and I bolt off to chemo driven by

Jonathan. I look at him, fist pump the air, laugh and alight the car with a 'party on Chemo!' He smiles at how mad I've become through all of this. 'Bat, shit, crazy,' he says.

Chemo is uneventful apart from my clockwatching. We have to be out of there and back to change for Kurran's sports day. The heat is rising and I find myself toxin-loaded, packet of skittles devoured and ready to come home for block two of my day.

After a quick wardrobe change, Kurran's sports day begins. Each house is marched out to a blaring 'Eye of the Tiger' which through the years has always made me giggle. Hulking 13-year-old, testosterone-fuelled lads with slightly hunched gaits trying desperately not to think of Sylvester Stallone on their last big sporting event at prep school definitely musters some sympathy from me.

My little sporting baby wins all his races. His hurdles, 100m (twice), takes lead in the relay and overall surprises his peers, teachers and parents alike. This is so worth how I'm feeling at the moment. And this must remain a secret (ahem). The 33 degrees is making me feel very nauseous which in turn makes me dizzy, exacerbated by the hairpiece that vows never to let my head breathe. Drinking lots of water to stay hydrated isn't quite cutting it, so after the last race I retire under a tree with Mum to some shady breeze.

My boy is so incredibly happy and when they ask the children to applaud their parents for their support and sitting out here in the heat, I see my youngest boy far in the distance raising his hands to applaud me. This, is worth the whole wide world and more.

As I ascend up the hill to get back to the car, my heavy legs and dizzy head are not giving me huge amounts of confidence. Then the vision of Jonathan carrying me up the hill in the middle of school, gives me the impetus of something out of Chariots of Fire. Back home, we have an hour before the next activity. I lay my head down for half an hour and this is all the power nap I need. Wardrobe change and out the door for his Leavers Play.

The two-hour play is a well-presented, humorous montage by the kids about their teachers and life at school. Many laughs are had, a video of their baby photos and the lads they have grown into, make us suitably emotional. And two hours later I emerge having thought I've lost my tailbone, but no it's intact just a bit sore. I cannot believe this is the end of an era. I never thought I would end eight years of school runs like this. But the most important thing I can muster is that I am here. I am alive and able to see my boy off into pastures anew. These are all gifts in life, only to be smiled at and cherished.

Sunday, 15 July, 2018 – Sleepless in Surrey

It's 3 am. I take a drug on the day of chemo and three days thereafter called Dexamethasone. It is a steroid designed to keep sickness at bay as well as my infamous allergic reactions. The problem is, though I take it no later than lunchtime, it keeps me up all hours of the night. Last week I averaged three hours sleep a night and during the day proceeded to talk like a parrot that had clearly disengaged its brain. As I say to my nurse who approves my chemo, I don't come up for air. I host lunch for friends, drive myself to chemo and back with Mum in tow, trips to London and for that I am so very grateful, but then I'm shattered. As she replies, people on their 5th cycle of Carboplatin shouldn't be able to function at this level.

Though this last couple of weeks, I've been up pontificating even on 'non-Dex' days. A suggestion that things are possibly playing on my mind. My seven-hour surgery and all the alleged complications that go with it notwithstanding, my campaign is also ever furrowing my brows.

I believe in chance. On Saturday, I had decided on an impromptu visit to my tennis club. I let the lovely Chairman who calls to check on me on the clubs' behalf know that I will pop in, though with not much notice. He's there with his cheery disposition to greet me but people have opted to stay home today. We settle into the clubhouse in a small group to watch the remainder of the men's Wimbledon semi-final. I have this knack of knowing instinctively when the ball is struck that it's going out and I'm very 'vocal' about it. My husband always says I'm quite 'put together' as a person, until I watch a sporting event, I'm passionate about. Whether it's tennis, cricket, rugby, athletics or even a World Cup in football (in that order), it turns me into a veritable hooligan. However, I do keep my composure at the club, though I really don't think Nadal should lose this match.

We all turn towards each other after the match to chat and inevitably arrive at the obvious, my condition. When I talk to people that don't know me, I tend to focus on my campaign here and in Pakistan. The Pakistan angle always warrants great interest and by chance, one gentleman in the group tells me he owns a radiography business and can put me in contact with two very large 'technology' companies in the region for potential data analytics. He does similar work in Qatar. I need data desperately. There is a denial amongst the local community about the reality of what is occurring. There is also an inherent rejection of all opinions coming from 'the outside'. I'm thrilled that a little unplanned trip to my tennis club can yield not only a lovely afternoon of tennis banter and laughter, but that it can generate such encouragement in an area I had not anticipated. My day's work is done.

Setting Up My Own Charity

Up at 3:30 am the following morning, this time having slept at 1:45 am. I look forward to 4:30 am when my husband will rise for work as always. Though if he peers in and sees I'm awake he brings me a lovely cup of Earl Grey while we chat. That is my positive start to the day. My husband and Earl Grey. It doesn't get better than that. After a Brexit chat and various other news that I've already caught up on for the last hour, we go through his schedule and discuss all things work, which I personally love to do. A welcome break from our 'surgical' conversations over the weekend.

Today we have a conference call with our lawyer. I am adamant about setting up my own charity rather than a fundraising 'social enterprise'. We are willing to kick start funding ourselves in order to be a registered charity in the UK, which has a base funding requirement. Then it's about a credible Board of Trustees and a list of donations we intend to make with entirely charitable intent. Social enterprises are allegedly less regulated and I want heavy regulation because with that comes a credibility towards my cause and intent. I will push on with my agenda. Though I'm trying to imagine how all this will fit like a seamless piece of the puzzle with my chemo and multiple surgeries to come. I feel myself once again, sauntering into the unknown.

Tuesday, 24 July, 2018 – A Meeting to Discuss My 'Life Altering Surgery'

Trepidation. After a full day of other appointments, I park outside my hospital and decide, despite the 30-degree heat, that I need to rest my head as my legs will simply not do the walking. I have a cool 40 minutes before I have to meet Jonathan for my appointment. I pay the parking, set my alarm and fall asleep on my special 'driving' pillow in the back seat of my car. I'm awoken by a loud knock and a quizzical but worried husband who has spotted the warden. 'She hasn't paid the ticket' he thinks. He approaches him asking why he is circling his car. 'There is a person asleep with all the windows shut inside your car, sir,' he replies. That old chestnut. I guess most people wouldn't leave their dogs in the car without a cracked window in 30-degrees. Fair play. Thank you, Mr Good Samaritan Warden. It's good to know strangers out there still care. Jonathan proceeds to wake me up as I jolt upright like a disturbed puppy (a little embarrassed) and kick into a strange kind of woozy gear. After two honey and oat biscuits dunked in some sweet Earl Grey tea in the waiting room, all is right with the world.

If I could bottle the amount of times, I've been told this surgery will change my life forever, well, I'd sell it for a fortune and probably cure cancer. I think as I embark into this new, unknown phase, the thing that amazes me is the unpredictability of it. I don't mean to be funny (okay well I do), but once you've had the tennis match that morphed in a day to a cancer diagnosis, then sepsis, then chemo, what you really want is a catalogue of the new and improved body you'll be flaunting around at 50. The problem with that is apparently something called a non-elective mastectomy.

Friday, 27 July, 2018 – The 'Elephant' In the Room

I love elephants. Always have, whether it's their regal strength yet sensitive disposition, their fight or flight juxtaposed with their need to rescue and love or their beautiful young. My father read *A Jungle Book* to me repeatedly as a child. My eyes would glaze wide as I leapt into the world of Mowgli and delighted in the march of the elephants. The vinyl would be on repeat all day. Although my most hated was *Trust in Me* by the snake "Kaa", so it would always be ceremoniously skipped and remained the least scratched and ironically untainted. As a highly sensitive child and adult, elephants fascinated me on all psychological realms. So, it loathes me to use this metaphor, except their presence is so large and magnanimous that to be in denial about having one in the room with you must take some phenomenal powers that be.

The physical shall be tended to by the country's best surgeon, plastic surgeon and oncologist team. The psychological is left solely for the person undergoing the mastectomy to fight. So why write this section of my blog? To give us all tools, awareness and the wherewithal to understand how best to emerge as different yet complete as we once were or perhaps never felt. From what I read, the emotional ripples of such a procedure run from a deep epicentre far and wide to a large circumference. Especially when it is a mandatory lifesaving exercise and not elective. Whether you start from the most intimate relationships, to wider familial or to a simple alienation from those walking across the street, effects have to be battled, even counteracted. This starts with awareness.

When I google sources these days, I stick to the medical, not the hypothetical conjecture that can be so damaging in the ether. A quick glance at the International Journal of Surgical Oncology yields a psychological study on women after a mastectomy. It talks about the three key pillars of psychology relating to this phenomenon.

One, a slightly odd notion of the 'fracture of the corporal imaginary'. This talks to the loss of a key organ in the body, which comes with low self-esteem and a certain avoidance of social relationships. The latter, for an extrovert like myself, would be a definite 'fracture' to be monitored at all costs.

Two, talks to the feeling of a loss of femininity relating to all things interpersonal such as one's closer relationships together with the intimacy involved. This red herring is even more critical to observe. Key relationships need protection but first, we have to realise those changes and embrace them.

Three, is the psychology of mutilation. Sounds harsh, but a true enough third pillar. Women are quoted as saying they would rather lose a hand than a 'hole' they cannot complete. While a psychological truth, I cannot simply accept this 'hole' and must make peace with the body I have and with its consequent loss as I know it.

I think about these things with the intention of taking them head-on, processing and dealing with them. These are psychological effects I want to pass through, not become. A tall order but not impossible. Such is the power of positive thinking.

In our modern and forward-thinking western culture, whether we are frolicking in the ocean with our toddlers, bikini-clad or going through childbirth with our husband's present, we have the freedom to be women. In many parts of the world, this would be considered a privilege, not a right. Yet historically, we have fought hard for our political and biological freedom as women and earned our rightful equality. The psychological effects of this procedure appear to threaten those liberties at the core. If we allow them to.

What does this mean for culture in Pakistan where there is less practice of "owning our femininity and sexuality"? One would assume less impact on core feminine values. I would hypothesise this not to be the case. This very idea that parts of our bodies are shrouded in secrecy (covering up all imagery innately feminine) could lead to a more secret self, thereby forcing a late detection of diseases like breast cancer. And therein, lies the problem.

There is definitely a cultural balance to be struck resulting in a psychologically optimal and healing response to discovering this disease. This needs to respect the culture and keep its integrity intact. A very difficult balance to strike.

Back in my doctor's meeting, I feel like a body reduced to a fractured image of a 'colour by numbers' self. As the solutions are described, I find myself reminded of one of those colouring books given to you as a child. Those with numbers to join, colours to code and lots of things to 'stick' on. From hair, accessories to clothing and in this case even body parts.

How am I going to put this positive theory into action today? I'm going to go and plant some flowers in the side of my garden border. It's frankly looking a bit sorry for itself with its shrivelled spring perennials (due to no rainfall). They shall be chosen, placed and coloured by numbers and I shall be in control of how beautifully my borders thrive.

Our Wedding Day, Cliveden House, June 3rd 2001

M and I, The Collection, Knightsbridge 1998

Our boys, Kurran and Kameron (left to right) 2018

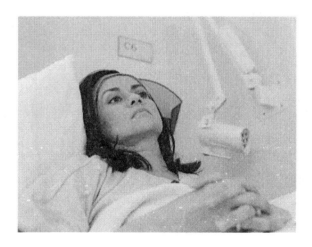

Chemotherapy, The Royal Marsden Hospital August 2nd, 2018

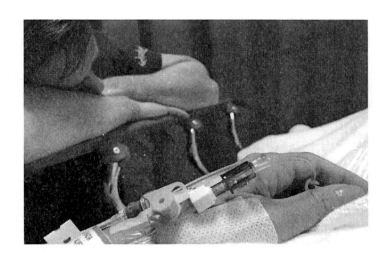

Rushed by ambulance to A&E with chest pains, June 2018
Radiotherapy, November 2018

Jonathan and I, St Georges Hill Tennis Club, circa 2015

My Mum and I, Gymkhana restaurant 2016

Modelling in Karachi, Pakistan, 1994

Modelling for my first cover of 'Fashion Collection', Karachi, Pakistan 1994

On the ramp for designer Shamael, Karachi, Pakistan 1994

Cover Shoots, Karachi, Pakistan 1994

Centrefolds, Karachi, Pakistan 1994

Fundraising in Justgiving campaign 'Lifting the Veil',
Marlborough College, 2018
Photograph by Sadia Barlow Photography
Makeup – Ambreen Makeup Artist

One week after sepsis, April 2018
Photograph by Sadia Barlow Photography
Makeup by Debbie Storey

Mum, my sister Sadia and I on my first birthday, Karachi Pakistan,
March 1972

Happy times, Menorca, Spain 2013

Breast Cancer Smiles

Logo design
Created by Sarah Brown as a donation for Justgiving

Thursday, 2 August, 2018 – The Blue Corridor

Finally, this day has arrived. The last Thursday I will spend the eight to nine hours that it takes to get through the process of being injected with copious amounts of drugs since March. I live in hope. Matt has a lovely, young energy. He is my cameraman for the day. He meets me at home to discuss our day at the hospital. We discuss the various options open to us, given we have not been allowed to film inside the hospital. So, Q&A it is. Together, we will have to weave a story on-site without the benefit of being able to dramatically show my last chemo. It was anything but dramatic. Sitting on a bench outside, I notice the leaves have started to brown and shed. Ironically, it isn't autumn yet, rather the heatwave that is creating that pre-winter crunch under my feet.

As he asks, I answer. Surprisingly, the words simply come. I alternate interviews between the very familiar process. Bloods, then meeting with the doctor, approval of chemo for the day, administration of chemo followed by the drive home. Even Mum is surprisingly natural in front of the camera. Matt is visibly moved. Because we are all speaking of matters from the heart.

There is a certain elation about having reached the last chemo. Never have I been so thrilled about so much cumulative poison going in my body, but it is important to finish the course. Important, if getting my cancer to retreat is of any significance. I am happy to see one of my favourite nurses on duty that day. She has always made it her business to get me out of there as fast as humanly possible. The other nurse is as surprisingly detached as this lady is interested. I take in chocolates and a card for the nurses and a separate one for the kitchen staff who have diligently served up multiple paninis and cups of tea throughout my time there. It's amazing how just some truffles and a card can cause so much delight. Yet they have no idea of my gratitude.

As the last doses pulse through my veins, I sleep like always when the pre-meds take their toll. As I awake, I look at my mum, sitting patiently and the last drip of Abraxane transfers itself through the tube into my body. One saline flush and it's over. At least for the time being, I tell myself. As I literally waltz out of the chemo ward (which sounds like it's been named after a resort in St Barts), I hug the nurses and wave goodbye until I pause at "The Blue Corridor".

There is a strange arrest that takes place. I have walked, sometimes stumbled up and down this corridor, for months. I think back to that last exam or last day at school or university and realise that this is not the same. At those times in life, I certifiably said goodbye. There was a certainty that I would never return. I realised I have no such surety here. I am likely to see "The Blue Corridor" again. I refrain from throwing that proverbial graduation cap in the air, for now.

There is a difference between being positive and lulling oneself into a false sense of security. I have triple negative breast cancer. It doesn't behave, isn't predictable and doesn't go away easily. For now, my chemotherapy is over and I can't wait to get it out of my body, even if just for a short time where I can enjoy feeling "normal". Normal that is, until September 5th, the date I've been given for my surgery.

Saturday, 4 August, 2018 – Olive trees, Rosemary, Jasmine and a special Celebration

Today, just two days after my last chemo, we will fly to the beautiful island of Menorca. We discovered it around eight years ago through my husband's love of boating that eventually became ours. For me, it is a connection with the ocean and the high reaching cliffs that etch the island's boundaries with such beauty. Being on the water gives me a sense of freedom as I bow to its vastness, power and control over my immediate world. To succumb to the power of the ocean is a beautiful thing – very different to succumbing to cancer which is something I refuse to do.

We are here to celebrate my husband's 50th. He has repeatedly deferred this to "next year" but deep down I am all about seizing the day and all those tired little clichés I swore I'd never, ever borrow. So, here it is, this is my carpe diem moment. Because, in my husband, I see plenty to celebrate, right here and right now. No 2019 projections allowed.

I have wondered since March whether I would make it to this week. It was pre-booked by family late last year when cancer was a ridiculous notion in our lives. I have wondered whether my chemo would be over, whether the cumulative effects would be too much for me to travel. Just whether I could join in celebrating the person who has been my rock for 19 years. And here I am. Small steps, little missions, all accomplished.

We arrive at our hotel, a beautiful 17th century Menorcan estate that has been converted into a haven lined with olive trees, beds of rosemary, sprouting jasmine each bursting with scents of all things Mediterranean. My love of olive trees has long rolled eyes in my family. It's my animated gesticulations of how vast their trunks are (indicating age), how gnarly their shape is (indicating rarity) and how beautifully they spring into the same fan-like shape (each olive branch indicating peace). I'm all smiles here.

It strikes me how happy these things now make me. How nature is just so powerful, be it ocean or land. In 1993, Menorca was declared a UNESCO biosphere reserve. The shorthand for this is that priority is given to the sustainability of the island's natural reserve and landscape.

My husband hates tomatoes. Yet I have never seen him devour a bruschetta with homegrown tomatoes, garlic, parsley and olive oil quite so fast. From fish extracted from the ocean to the natural produce of the land, free of pesticides and chemicals, a sense of well-being begins to permeate the body and senses. It leaves its sister islands Majorca and Ibiza behind, flailing in the distance like wannabe cousins. We love our little, hidden jewel in the Mediterranean.

Moving on from the Menorcan sales pitch, Jonathan's sisters and their families have arrived. We are all set for a family celebration. I've ordered flowers and candles for the table and purchased as many embarrassing table decorations our local nonstop party shop could offer. The crew and host for our boat excursion the following day has been booked. Turning half a century is not to be let off lightly.

Organising events and occasions has always been my thing. But for now, I'm focused on making memories. As my husband calls them, moments that matter. The Rosé has flowed, the local fish, vegetables, bread, olive oil, cheese have all been plentiful. We finish with a hazelnut cream cake alight with candles and other celebratory signs. The event manager has added a second identical cake when she realises I have too many decorations that wouldn't fit on just one. As a result, we have more moments that matter.

The bits that are a surprise? I suppose I'm not as well as I would have liked. The chemo is at its most cumulative. I'm not allowed in the sun because it interacts with the chemo. I'm not allowed in the water for fear of picking up an infection. My husband's family help me walk to the car because my fingers and toes are constantly numb, making it hard to balance on the plethora of wedges that I refuse not to wear. I fight my inner perception that I currently resemble a 90-year-old, which brings all sorts of metaphoric 'mutton dressed as lamb' analogies in my slightly crazy head. I manage to attend lunches before a rest at the hotel and I am at all the dinners. But I can't launch into my beloved ocean, snorkelling and mono-skiing as I've always done.

The next day, a wonderful day on the water has been had by all. We sit on the bow, just my husband and I, as we listen to the chatter and excited shrieks behind us, as our family are having the time I have hoped for. We look on to our favourite Cala. A place we have anchored and spent nights under the stars, in candlelight. Mornings we have woken, sipped our Earl Grey and dived straight into the clear, turquoise ocean. A place that, for this moment, is just ours. A few tears roll for both of us, but I end with a note of gratitude. I tell him how thankful I am for the 19 years I've spent, blissfully happy with him. Nothing and no one can take that away. This is our time to smile.

Saturday, 18 August, 2018 – Waiting for the Chemo to Leave

Back down to earth with a thud. My surgery date is drawing closer. Weeks on, the chemo is still going strong. My face now has a rash that itches and irritates as it swells up almost balloon-like. I'm assuming this is a withdrawal from all the drugs (steroids, antihistamines, anti-sickness) that I have now stopped taking. My nails have turned yellow and bruised as they provide dubious cover for my numbed fingers. There is pus seeping out from underneath three of them. These are the nails I will probably lose. The eyelashes that I have thanked the powers above for keeping have now started to shed. I thought it would all be long gone now, but the chemo is not letting up. Maybe it's doing the same with my cancer, who knows?

I'm conscious that each day the chemo persists is a day I won't feel normal. To add insult to injury, it has been announced to me that I'm not an 'ideal' candidate for the DIEP flap surgery. In short, this is a surgery whereby they will take tissue from my stomach (through a hip-bone to hip-bone incision) and replace the implant that will be put in temporarily. I don't have much of this tissue and certainly none to waste. This is good news. The bad news is, because I have such little available tissue, a temporary implant will need to be in for a year. Why a year? Because I need radiotherapy which apparently shrinks and somewhat destroys whatever lies in its wake. One year from my radiotherapy (which is scheduled after my op recovery this year), I will have the DIEP flap operation. I see the logic in all of this but the emotions are saying 'are you kidding me right now?' After recovery from that, there will be a third surgery to apply "finishing touches".

When this is announced to us, my husband and I stare at each other in disbelief as we are taken through to 2020 in one short, fell swoop. Furthermore, this is all just talking about my "cosmetic completion". What we are not comprehending is the pathology that is far more critical in September 2018. This will form the prognosis for my cancer. The road just got one hell of a lot longer with our collective fingers crossed. It's 16 days after my last chemotherapy and I'm still waiting for its departure.

Thursday, 23 August, 2018 – When a Type of Cancer is Taboo...

taboo: təˈbuː /

noun

1. 1

a social or religious custom prohibiting or restricting a particular practise or forbidding association with a particular person, place, or thing.

Adjective

2. 1

prohibited or restricted by social custom.

verb

3. 1

place under a taboo.

In my humble opinion, the word "breast" isn't covered by any of these definitions. Except in some parts of the world. Therein lies the problem. Though the hypocrisy isn't lost on me, it's a body part good enough to feed and nourish the very beings that ultimately deign it "taboo". More on this later but for this week, surgery looming, I thought it better to have a few laughs at what constitutes certain cancer responses that should be "prohibited by social custom".

I'm not an angry person by nature. I tend to stay quiet when something offends me, to a point. Obviously, I know how to stand up for myself...eventually, but sometimes internally I choose just to have a giggle, a smile or just feel plain bemused. Very few of the things that people have said to me since I've had cancer have made me react, but they have achieved all of the above emotions at one time or another. I'll start with the first one that is surprisingly common.

Number 1

'I have an aunt, that has a daughter in her 40s and her best friend had breast cancer. Her treatment was really awful, took two years. Took it out of her I tell you.'

'I'm sorry to hear that.' Shocked, inquisitive face. 'How is she now?' my eyes wide expecting stories of remission and well-being.

'Oh, she died six months ago...'

No word of a lie. Not only have I experienced this, I've heard of many cancer patients who experience the same thing. There's no coming back from this one.

Number 2

Enter the drycleaners minding your own business. Lady behind the counter says, 'You look different.'

And there it is. Drops off a cliff. No qualifier to be seen, no explanation for this statement. Are we talking Atila the Hun "different" or Megan Fox "different'? Given my wig, scaling skin and bruised nails, I'm guessing not the latter. I smile awkwardly but can't wait to exit stage left.

Number 3

'Chemo is a scam. I prefer homoeopathy myself.'

This coming from someone who has never had cancer. The person prefers homoeopathy when there's no life at stake to gamble with. Do they prefer it because they believe in its high confidence statistics on cancer survival, or because it involves fewer side effects? The jury is out on this curious point of view from the opinionated non-cancerous person. Moving swiftly along.

Number 4

'Marijuana is all you need to cure cancer.' Think we might be talking about a cure for the emotional doldrums here. The suggestion is to go and smoke a few doobies then see if those cancer cells do a runner. Risky strategy much?

Number 5

On a consent form, pre-CT scan, having been in the hospital with sepsis for most of March, a nurse cheerily asks: 'Is there any chance you could be pregnant?'

My thoughts? *Yes, I'm having triplets and I just got an offer from Elite model agency. Not.*

Number 6

'You look better without hair,' said no one ever. Oh, but they did. All intention being good I understand; it is simply the most unconvincing pep talk I have ever received.

Number 7

Initial health professional, who shall remain nameless, not part of my amazing team: 'The bad news is, you have triple negative breast cancer. The good news is, I'm going to sort you out with gorgeous little "B" cups.' I have no words.

Number 8

Upon break-up with a god-awful chauvinist boyfriend, my employee tucks into a large plate of mayonnaise-clad pasta. I routinely ask how she is this week.

'Feeling very nauseous all the time. Not got much appetite. Just putting one foot in front of the other every day I guess.'

I've just arrived back from my 16th chemo session...rolling eye emoji.

These should feature on the next *People say the funniest things*. There are some true humdingers out there, but the word "breast" isn't one of them. Back in my home country of Pakistan, we need a crest of change in the perceptions towards breast cancer. We need to create the emotional permission for these women to get treated early. Surely anyone dying un-necessarily at this rate is an issue for the global community?

Wednesday, 5 September, 2018 – The Surgery 'Drive Thru'

If it's possible to be in a "I just lost my breast" funk and hardly think about it, that's where I've been for a bit. That said, I have connected with the phenomenal pain that is four procedures…through delightful amounts of codeine. However, I'm finally come around to persisting with my mission so I shall press on.

I imagine myself at one of those American "drive-throughs". Perhaps because it feels just this impersonal or maybe just this ridiculous but here goes…

In an automated American accent:

'Good morning, ma'am, what can I get for you today?'

'Err, can I have one mastectomy with immediate reconstruction please?'

'Sure, would you like silicone or saline with that?'

'Err, silicone please.'

'No problem, ma'am. Can I get you anything else today?'

'Yes, could I also have a left reduction as well as a right axillary (lymph node) clearance and a portocath removal please?'

'Sure no problem, ma'am. That will be $46.99. Please move forward to the next window. Y'all have a nice day!'

What's my point here? I suppose it's the juxtaposition between something that sounds like a nonchalant fast-food order and the reality that strikes the person heading to that "next window". Usually pain, recovery, more treatment and then a big, fat question mark.

That morning I awake in a twilight zone. My mum and husband are probably bemused by my "normal" demeanour yet aware that I might "lose the plot" at any point, given that

I haven't so far. The latter does not occur. There is a strange comfort when you rock up to the Royal Marsden hospital, even for this. I take solace in its towering, historically successful presence. We're the first people in the surgical unit that morning. I'm taken into a small private room where I change into my gown (to my best friend M, do you remember our Balenciaga gown joke when you were in hospital? – well I'm wearing one of those). M is here with me too. Her necklace is in my bag and her spirit is guiding me. I have my two unwavering supporters outside. My mum and husband sit waiting, strung out with considerably more worry and sadness than myself. My surgeon enters and does some colour-by-numbers drawing on my body. When she is happy, my plastic surgeon arrives to add to this inevitable work of art. My prayer for that is hopefully an acceptable body without cancer in it.

Once prepped, they are ready for me. I feel like I've cheerfully accepted that I'm going to a chamber for a lethal injection. The two nurses take us all down to the basement not unlike being escorted to the dungeons of the Tower of London. I'm still chatting and smiling wondering if Henry VIII's wives had this demeanour on their way to the tower. I hug my husband and Mum goodbye at some double doors marked 'Surgery – no admission beyond this point'. Question, why the hell are they allowing me in then? I see my mum's face begin to crumble. That is a cue not to look at my husband, so I just keep walking.

As I lie down on the anaesthesia table, everyone is prepping various parts of me. It is surreal to be surrounded by complete strangers during the last conscious moments of an apparently "life-changing surgery". They are very kind, but then so is my stylist before a haircut. Before I ponder this weirdness too long, something delightful courses through my veins and I say I'm feeling drowsy. They are pleased that the pre-med relaxants are working. I could use these on holiday with my kids. Fantastic way to actually have one! Fade to black.

Fast forward four hours to the recovery room, I awake in a complete anaesthetic haze. Directly across, I spot a jolly old gentleman who is tucking into sandwiches while chatting away to the staff, straight out of some Enid Blyton novel. I hear the muffled sounds of my surgeon assuring me the surgery went well, wait, what was that last thing? There was more cancer found in my lymph nodes than expected? They took out more? Hmmm, shall verify later minus the morphine.

After what seems an eternity, three hours later than expected, I'm wheeled into my room. There is a dish in our part of the world which translates quite literally to fried brain or 'bheja fry'. My husband and mum look like they're owning that title right now. I feel somewhat out of my senses and can't move my chest or arms, restricted and somewhat uncomfortable. This is not so bad surely? 'Wait till the meds wear off' says evil person on left shoulder, smoking a cigarette with glee. (Metaphorically, evil character has evil accessories in my imagination). Still wonderfully drowsy my unstoppable chatter takes a few hours to return. So does the pain.

Pre-empting my horror (for fear that I might find out alone later through my social media), my husband tells me Rachael Bland has passed away. Surely not September 5th? This was a date etched in my mind as the day that changed everything, and here is one more devastating thing it changed. This wonderful lady that has given me so much strength not just during my ordeal but on this day, is no more. Rachael Bland has become quite the household name recently. Her plight of taking the taboo out of cancer and essentially putting the 'Can' back in it, has reached phenomenal heights. She and I had the same diagnosis (triple negative breast cancer), a very similar treatment plan, a love of holidaying in Menorca (not least) and September 5th now bearing such significance. Only she was deemed terminal recently. She had reached out to me a couple of weeks ago to talk on her podcast about cultural differences surrounding breast cancer. It was never to transpire. I try and let her sad demise, as well as the surgery I've just had, sink in.

I think I have quite a good pain threshold, but after a couple of days, even I reach for the morphine. The surgery itself has gone well, in that the procedure has gone to plan. Finding more lymph nodes with cancer and then doing a clearance around them, not so much. We will wait 10 days for the pathology results. They have done exactly what they were supposed to do and done it well I'm told.

I spend a couple of days at the Royal Marsden hospital which lives up to its name in every way. A real gold standard in cancer treatment. The following morning, I try to sit up and do my arm exercises collapsing nauseous and dizzy. The nurse forces me up, makes me breathe deep and solves the problem. I force the issue as I contemplate the apparent horrors of lymphedema as a tennis player. Clever ladies these nurses. Time to go home for an unexpected, week long, "what the hell just happened" funk.

The messages from friends and family pour in. This is a hard one for people even in the West, so no wonder it's proving near impossible in Pakistan. Most are carefully crafted messages of support, others, quite simply say, 'One or two mastectomies?', or 'this will be the easiest thing you will go through in all of your treatment.' Well, they make it to my blog with a wink emoji. Now lies the wait for the pathology results on September 17th.

Monday, 17 September, 2018 – The Pathological Truth

I've come across the phrase 'it's ok not to be ok' many times recently. I couldn't agree more. But is it okay to *be* okay throughout your breast cancer ordeal ("journey", my sweet ass!)? I think the latter may be more controversial. Is it okay that I have listened to my invasive cancer diagnosis without a tear in sight, thrown no tantrums, walked nonchalantly through surgery doors and then stared into space when I'm told my treatment plan just extended itself to 2020? Is it okay to smile or is the word "psychotic" coming to mind?

I can feel psychologists grinding their teeth and rubbing their hands with glee in the ether. Those close to me would have previously deemed me too sensitive, needing a thicker skin, unable to watch suffering of any kind. Then what is it with my own? I seem to be fine with it. I can hear words bandied about as I write: "denial", "coping mechanism", "emotional shutdown", hell even "bat shit crazy" I suppose whatever title we choose to give it, however, we get through our nightmares, it's got to be okay, right?

Rewind to last week and my pathology result. I will admit it's been a little hard to write. When your pain is only punctuated by marginal pain relief, denial doesn't come so easily. Then revisiting the facts by trying to craft every word is like plunging your head into a vat of hot oil or poking needles in one's proverbial eye – you catch my gist. Still, I relent.

I'm on antibiotics as one of my multiple "wounds" is seeping a green substance which I'm told is not an infection but we are acting with caution. Mr Pico, as I affectionately call my buzzing, flashing Tamagotchi-type dressing is with me for another week. This is clever, negative pressure wound therapy which promotes healing through vacuum-packed bandaging while preventing infection.

Back at Cancer Headquarters, aka the Royal Marsden, it's an hour-long wait. My surgeon is wonderfully patient and never rushes you out of the room. Being a glass half full type or let's say glass completely overflowing type, I take solace in this fact. However, I will admit my body is so tense that my right arm is irretrievably glued to my side putting the Queen's Guard to shame.

I know bits and pieces of what is coming. For example, I know at the time of surgery, I had two clipped lymph nodes with a tumour detected by scans. I was told afterwards that two more have been found. Now I'm told in total, three have microscopic amounts of cancer in them, while one has well…rather a lot more. This, after five months of aggressive chemotherapy. There has been a 90% clearance of the cancer via chemo and now the remaining 10% has been allegedly gouged out via mastectomy and an axillary lymph node clearance. I say allegedly because my group risk for "recurrence and/or death" just got higher. Not getting that remission glass of champagne out yet. This makes me eligible for a one-month-long daily round of radiotherapy and a further six months of an oral chemotherapy drug called

Capecitabine. Tear check for any little, pathetic, salty escapee, negative. Though an irritable "Oh FFS!" does run through the brain. This is a healthy sign of lurking emotion as I'm not a habitual swearer.

I consider 90% a good result. Think GCSE. This would be a fist pump moment. Err, you're a 47-year-old with cancer, you crazy idiot, not a 16-year-old with a UCCA form. Apparently, a complete pathological clearance of the cancer was expected prior to surgery. I can sense this in my bones and Google confirms it. Google, the search engine that never did any good news bring. In medical terms, any triple negative cancer over 5cm (mine was 10) with nodal involvement (sounds so romantic) after chemo makes you a contender for further treatment. In other good news, I've got "more than 5mm" clearance.

I choose not to see this whole prognosis as scraping the bottom of the positivity barrel, but actually just not the ideal scenario we were hoping for. 'There are people far worse off love, so stay in your box' says the inner voice that I would like to shoot sometimes. While we're at it, could someone please remove the phrase 'It is what it is' from our vernacular replacing it with 'It is what it bloody shouldn't be.' Many thanks. And that there, is a neat little summation of my pathological truth.

Monday, 1 October, 2018 – Rehabilitation and Radiotherapy

I've had many people point out how much easier radiotherapy is than chemo. Terms like 'a walk in the park', 'painless', 'like you've sunbathed too long' have been frequently used to respond to my qualms. Being me, I tend to latch on to positives like my life depends on it and run with the vibe to get my nerves through to the other side.

There is one small issue. These helpful tips have not been formulated as a result of major surgery that includes axillary lymph node clearance. They've usually involved someone's surgically untouched, excuse my language, testicles. This is not a parallel universe. As I've found out in physiotherapy, which has now become a must, my right arm is feeling a bit put out frankly. It's irritation with having one too many lymph nodes cleared out is being expressed with tight cording of the muscles and a reluctance to well, move. The pain on the left is negligible. One tick. The pain on the right has a whole pain management team at the Royal Marsden working on it. Who knew? I had no idea there was such a specialisation and if they are trying to become my new BFF, this is a fine way to start. The problem is, for my planning meeting and scan on Friday 5th October, I will need to hold my arm above my head on and off for over 30 minutes. This position will then need to be repeated in each radiotherapy session. This seems like a sick joke at the moment because I can't get it 90 degrees perpendicular to my body without wincing.

Upon examination, it becomes apparent that I have no reflexes in my knees ankles or feet. I also have nerve ending damage in my fingertips and toes. I'm loathed to disrespect "Mr Chemo" here but frankly, there is a bit of resentment developing. He should have been satisfied with taking my hair. Now steps need to be taken to grow new nerves and apparently there is a topical cream for this. Furthermore, given that I have fewer lymph nodes and more swelling on my right side, drainage becomes long and cumbersome. Not to mention the nerves that have been severed in my arm. The remaining army of lymph nodes is protesting and for that we have "Super Pain Relief Hero". A tablet that deals with nerve pain whilst making me slightly giddy. At last, we have a credible Rosé replacement! I'm back in a virtual reality of Party Central apart from the three sets of exercises I have to do to get through planning on Friday.

Meanwhile, in my "life since cancer", hair is making its re-appearance on my head, eyelashes and eyebrows. In my dreams, this sits in close competition with a budget-less jaunt down Bond Street. Only the hair return is winning. Kind of. The minuscule hairs on my legs are wondering why I'm ruthlessly waxing them away. Sorry guys, but after months of feeling like Danny Devito's ugly sister, you puppies haven't got a hope in hell. A wax strip hath no fury like a woman scorned by the curse of masculinity. I'm not just embracing but tightly hugging every girlie bone in this body. I've never been a "bow and sweetheart" type, but I find myself wondering if a bad impression of a sorority sister is just what the doctor ordered. In pursuit of my more feminine side, my style stakes are becoming frighteningly low.

To digress further, I'm reading a mind-blowing book called *When Breath Becomes Air* by Paul Kalanithi. Published posthumously, I had originally thought it might have a detrimental effect on my albeit irritating but "smiley" outlook. I have read half the book in one night. It is a compulsive, stunning read. The author was not only a promising neurosurgeon of the highest calibre but a writer whose words flow like a meaningful river of beauty. He makes poetry out of living in the face of death. A lesson, I feel, should be lost on no one. Just the foreword from his friend releases a reluctant tear.

"Be ready. Be seated. See what courage sounds like. See how brave it is to reveal yourself in this way. But above all, see what it is to still live, to profoundly influence the lives of others after you are gone, by your words."

Abraham Verghese, Foreword 'When Breath Becomes Air'.

Thursday, 4 October, 2018 – Lifting the Veil off Asian breast cancer

Amongst Asian women, deep under the guise of a prolific disease, amidst many issues, there lies a certain problem. A problem that may be killing them. The guise is breast cancer, the problem is shame.

There are many reasons why Asian women in both their indigenous abodes and abroad are struggling with breast cancer. To name a few, a lack of awareness, a lack of financial support, a lack of medical infrastructure and also, a lack of cultural permission.

It is the latter issue that I choose to focus upon. There are many efforts in place to address funding, access to treatment and medical advances being made to progress the mortality rate downwards. However, one of the statistics that is uniformly alarming is that women are presenting their condition at too late a stage. This culminates in a higher mortality rate for this group. A lack of awareness is partly to blame but there is much evidence to support the fact that neither the breast nor its cancer is an acceptable public subject matter within the Asian culture.

Understandably, this is a massive leap that can't be made overnight. We are simply not going to change the vernacular so deeply ingrained in a culture without unseating beliefs held very dear and deep to all. However, we can start the conversation, we can ask the questions and we can protest the values that prevent women from living their lives to the fullest possible degree.

I choose to do this by example. I'm an Asian woman living in Britain who has (despite my natural instincts to remain private) exposed my story in an online blog, accessible to all. I am telling my tale however personal, however difficult. I have shared images of my hairless head. Hair, a stratospheric symbol of femininity as catalogued by its importance in the culture. I am doing it with a smile indicative of an attitude that is possible even with breast cancer. If I can, surely all Asian women out there have the ability to rise up, take charge and own their livelihood.

She can start by looking for the following signs and symptoms to report immediately:

- A lump or area that feels thicker than the rest of the breast
- Redness or rash on the skin, on or around the nipple
- A change in size or shape
- A change in skin texture (puckering or dimpling)
- Change in the nipple's position or shape
- Any liquid emission from the nipple
- Persistent pain in the breast or armpit

- Swelling in the armpit or collarbone

In doing this, she can begin her journey towards life again with her head held high.

Monday, 15 October, 2018 – Death begins with "D"

It's the ultimate fear. It is the very thing we battle when we "fight or flight". It's the great leveller. It knows no status, it understands no age and it always arrives uninvited. It's death. And we don't like to talk about it.

I've always said I would find it far harder to be left behind than to go. What does our existence really mean and why are we so afraid of not existing?

Almost one year ago, on November 7th, 2017, I lost a friend that I had known for 31 years. I had depended on her always being there, background or foreground it simply didn't matter. Her presence in my life was calming, nurturing, a tonne of fun and about as down to earth as it got. She was one of those friends where 'no one else would do'. In the past ten years, since having children I had developed all sorts of anxieties such as a fear of flying, a fear of not being the driver in a car, a fear of heights; the list was building. The day I saw her three weeks after her death, the day before her funeral with the casket accidentally open, my fear of death disappeared. To this day, I don't fully understand why. All I know is, I faced my fears that day.

Is one's existence greater in life, or is it greater in death? If you answered 'obviously in life', then how is it that someone who has passed can still impact one's response to a life-threatening disease? How can they still whisper in our ear, lift one's spirits, impart their wisdom and be omnipresent in your life? That is the legacy they call love and it certainly transcends life.

I have recently listened to many conversations about wills, estates and other alleged legacies, all in the context of poor familial bonds, many broken relationships and a great dearth of self-esteem. The truth is that if you have not found peace within yourself, if you have not processed your inner demons, no will, estate or monetary legacy is ever going to complete the empty you. Someone asked me recently, why I seem so "okay" with the subject matter of death (not to be confused with being "okay" with dying). My answer was not, 'because I don't feel loved', my answer was, 'because I do'.

I truly believe our legacy is the bank of memories we provide, the feeling of love we impart and the life that we continue to breathe into people long after we are gone.

Friday, 26 October, 2018 – Through the Radiotherapy Glass

04:49. It's true, I write the most when I sleep the least. I suppose the writing comes when one lies there with nothing but thoughts. Gone are the iPhones, the glare of the television, the rays of light from romantically hued lampshades and all the things that create such stunning distractions throughout our time awake. Thoughts are what we have left. Thoughts and a very stiff arm that I've been trying to stretch for the last hour.

I have perhaps left a few blank pages in between my musings about death and my preparation for radiotherapy. It has taken two CT scans to get through the planning phase. "Planning" is the word assigned to the process of defining where the rays go to walk the path of least destruction. The greater good in other words. From that light "brush" past my heart, I'm told, to the second CT scan that is required because I didn't hold my breath the first time to ensure least lung damage.

Apparently, what is also integral to planning is…wait for it, "tattoos", the radiographer says. I am looking at her like she has five heads. The one thing I have meticulously avoided my whole life; that which I am ridiculously prudish about is what I'm now being force-fed. I didn't throw tantrums as a child but inside my head I'm jumping up and down like a two-year-old having my first throw-your-toys-out-of-pram tantrum. I. Don't. Want. Tattoos. All they see is my compliant smile (this one is about the most artificial I can muster). They really don't want to hear what I'm calling them in my head. Fake, wide, toothy smile emoji.

The end result has me giggling. Four tiny dots to permanently mark the range of the beams. An exercise in minimal pointillism rather than a full-blown Van Gogh, I contain my inner horror. And on they go, four little pinpricks filled with permanent ink. I remind myself of the surgery I had six weeks ago, scars and all, so as to shut down my inner tattoo diva. What amazes me is the normality with which we undergo these procedures. When in that predicament, this really is your "new normal", that's the buzz word in cancer circles nowadays.

My physio has been singularly aimed at enabling my arm to stay up in stirrups during my "treatment". My use of inverted commas throughout this piece is not a happy accident. These are words that embody new meaning. In my previous life, treatment meant an oxygenated facial or some aroma-filled reflexology. This is a far cry from it, but it still sounds gloriously indulgent. That irony makes me grin. Grin with mischief, rather than smile with poetry. I digress.

Day One of 15 arrives. Thankfully, Jonathan is around to see me through the initial trepidation of said new treatment. This is a huge comfort to me as for some reason he will be why the rays only eradicate any leftover cancer cells. They will not touch my heart because he has that.

The radiotherapy department has been dug deep into the ground where it opens out into an abyss of columns, atriums and waiting areas for each machine I have been assigned to "Cedar". This is phonetically the start of my dearest friend M's surname. She's still watching over me and in control of my well-being, but then she always was. As my name is called, I am shown in, to a door that looks like it will lead to great things but in true Alice in Wonderland style, it's just a tiny cubicle with a mirror, a chair and a pile of gowns. In my sartorial splendour, I open a door on the other side that leads to something out of a sci-fi film. *Curiouser and Curiouser.* More Alice references.

As I'm lead through corridors full of radiation warnings, we enter Cedar which looks like something out of a Star Wars movie, only I've never fancied being Princess Leia. I've always failed to understand men's universal fascination with this (frankly rather plain) woman complete with ridiculous buns on either side of her head. Still, I'm all gowned up, tatted and ready for the role, short of the buns, you understand.

As I lie there with my arms in stirrups staring up at the machine, my eyes can't help but dart around spotting the blue beams that run over my body like some high-tech target practice for an assassin. Oh, the irony. The radiographers engage in some foreign language while they prod to get me into the correct position to the millimetre before they proceed to have a fun game of noughts and crosses all over my chest with blue pens. I have decided radiographers have a sensitivity chip missing. This hits me, particularly when one mistakes my stomach for a side table on which to rest her very sharp pointy file about an inch from my incisions. When I flinch, she tells me to be still. 'Breast-cancer-smiles' is about to turn into 'breast-cancer-murders'.

They announce they are leaving the room to start my treatment. What is very clear is that if they stayed and held my hand as their day job, they'd be dead as a doornail in the not too distant future. Toddler not happy about being left behind. I hear the words 'breathe in, breathe out' over the loudspeaker twice before I'm told to hold my breath for 20 seconds while the machine whirls over my head making a buzzing noise. I smile again as I think of the deep irony between breath and no breath. The difference between life and death. This is totally lost on these two, which in all fairness is probably appropriate given the madness that is their day job. In a few breathes, stop breathing repeats, it's over. Until tomorrow, when Cedar and I will meet again.

Wednesday, 31 October, 2018 – A Fundraising Campaign to 'Lift the Veil'

Someone said to me recently 'love him or hate him, Imran Khan never gives up. Every time he gets knocked down, he gets back up again…and that is the key to his success.'

It is amazing how hard it is to reach out to person after person and get no response. But the ones that do respond truly humble you. I must come clean and confess I'm a really terrible narcissist. My sister is my witness. I call her the "Insta nag" in my life. To be fair, she is a huge supporter so it's all in my interest but holy mother, can I not get this Instagram thing down. Give me a keyboard and I'll go hell for leather, but an iPhone with a camera pointing at myself to share all my innards with the world – this is my idea of hell. Then I try and make every post meaningful, so I'm not wasting people's time. I'm told this is not the point. Apparently, people want to follow your daily life, from the outfits to the pouts to the party nights that should never have been recorded. It's a voyeurs' world. If it hadn't been for my cause, I would have stayed an Instagram virgin.

The idea for this campaign did not come from the dynamic that is Instagram. 'Lifting the Veil' was inspired by the need to be authentic. When trying to communicate that there is "no shame" in breast cancer to the Asian community, I found myself grappling with language because rather startlingly, it translates as "shameless" (*besharam*) which has only negative connotations. It was at that point I realised that shame in South Asian culture is seen as a good thing. The second penny that dropped was that the word "breast" doesn't exist in the language. So how on earth do you say 'there is no shame in breast cancer'?

There are certain things that are very definitive about South Asian culture. Youth, health and indeed hair play a very large part in an Asian woman's self-esteem. I currently have none of those things. I decided that was the very reality I needed to expose – that it is acceptable to be me. My "unveiling" is supposed to represent the tangible reality of being a woman with breast cancer in Asian skin. The idea dramatizes four powerful metaphors. The bridal feel represents youth, the adornments are all things Asian, the hairlessness is cancer and lifting the veil, the taboo. Because there is no shame in breast cancer.

Then comes generosity of spirit. My sister and her husband harness their incredible photographic talent. Our sons' school generously provides a beautifully British backdrop in contrast to all things Asian. Ambreen, a renowned makeup artist donates a member of her team to do my makeup. I turn up as the case in point and hopefully you have a visually, powerful message.

I am unaware at this point that I will raise £4000 in just the two months to come towards efforts in South Asia. This has to be worth the exposure to all things narcissistic. I hold up my hands and bow to Instagram.

Tuesday, 13 November, 2018 – The Three Teddy Bears

"We don't see things the way they are. We see them as we are." Anais Nin

Originally, if I had one word to describe going through radiotherapy it would be *frigid* as derived from *Frigidaire*. In other words, cold as opposed to the rays that represent all things hot. My love affair with being microwaved on a daily basis for three weeks never quite got off to a flying start. Though my opinion went full circle.

Emotions have run high during this period. Who knew reading through cancer leaflets would be my new recreational pastime. I'm not going to break any records for most exciting extracurricular activity. Anyway, said leaflets on radiotherapy advise that apparently, this is not unusual. As it is often the last part of treatment, there are apparently feelings of fear and abandonment. Though I have no such issues. This process can leave at its earliest convenience, thank you. Nor, is it the last part of my treatment. Double irritation.

From being poked and prodded with cold hands, listening to sweet nothings such as abbreviations like '1mm sup' and '0.5mm inf' to chest burning sensations and nausea, I have just about had my fill. 'Sup' is short for superior meaning towards the head. 'Inf' means inferior so towards the feet. Directional specification of the beams is measured to the last fraction of a millimetre.

The weekends off have been a welcome break. It is one weekend in between that I'm very kindly invited to a lunch at my tennis club. I'm eager to catch up with old faces if not a little bit anxious. I'm reminded of the fact that as I hobble to the clubhouse because of the neuropathy in my feet (nerve death due to chemo causing numbness and pain) I resemble the Granny that my years do not suggest.

I'm welcomed with applause which touches me instantly. I have a seat saved and a wonderful Sunday roast to look forward to. One hangover from boarding school is that I love school dinner-type food such as overcooked vegetables and gravy from granules. But only on a roast dinner plate. Strange but true and this may never be repeated. Questions are firing and I answer to the best of my ability. Everyone is warm, chatty and supportive, bar the one lady sitting next to me. She is eerily quiet. She speaks very little as she works her way through her food. She asks no questions of me, makes no comments and offers no words of comfort. I continue in my usual upbeat fashion. Once their questions are answered, I relish hearing about their lives and how "normal" once felt. In the middle of dessert, said lady abruptly puts down her fork and announces she is leaving. With that, she exits about as fast as her 70-something legs can carry her. We all look around with the 'is it something I said?' look.

All becomes clear when someone volunteers that her daughter (around my age) died of cancer. My instant feeling is guilt. Guilt for having answered the questions, guilt for talking about cancer, guilt for being positive, guilt for still being alive when her daughter is not.

In contrast, the following week is M's first death anniversary. A day that feels emotional from the moment I wake up. Thankfully, three of us, some of her closest friends decide to get together that day after my radio session. We share untold stories, marvel at her mad sense of humour and know that she would be sitting right next to us if life had taken a different turn. We don't need an anniversary to remember her by, but there is something deeply comforting about the stories we tell while just being together.

They are asking questions about me now. My one friend relates to my treatment and offers advice and insight. It is at this point a powerful realisation comes my way. She too lost her daughter to cancer. Her daughter was four. I remember the devastation well. Yet, she is sensitive, kind and one of the bravest women I know. She never once makes me feel guilty for surviving another 43 years.

This takes me back to the Anais Nin quote. Cancer is cancer and death is death. But don't we all process it so differently? We are simply not meant to lose our children and

I believe that is a type of grief second to none. The contrast of the two reactions strikes me at a very deep level. No judgement, just observation.

I am further reminded of my friend when in a rare moment of feeling a bit sorry for myself during my radiotherapy, I glance up at the glass disc delivering the rays. I notice three teddy bear stickers staring back at me. I'm instantly put in my place as I realise, they are there to pacify very small children that lie in my place. There is nothing that brings you down to earth with a bigger thud.

On my last day, I exit Cedar, as my machine is affectionately named, to find a young girl who has been a rare familiar face waiting for me. She wants to say goodbye and wish me luck. With quivering lips, I thank her and exit stage left into the little cubicle room before I'm caught out. I manage to lock the door as my floodgates open. At last, the tears that have eluded me roll down my face like some tardy, frustrated jailbirds delighted to have been let out of prison. I might just be human and not a robot after all. So this undoes my entire take on radiotherapy as ironically this girl achieves the completely impossible. She finally makes me cry. From cold to hot in one fell swoop. We really do see things the way we are.

Sunday, 25 November, 2018 – Cyber Crime and The Talking Tree

The talking tree is me. More on that madness later. In the cancer newsroom, there are only the dreary side effects of radiotherapy to report. Shooting pains that punctuate your day like rude interruptions. A constant burning that feels like you've had a fight with an incinerator coupled with copious amounts of pain relief. Two weeks post, the skin and tissue resemble a snare drum that has been flambéed. Not the most appetising of metaphors but it is what comes to mind. I'm told this could last a while as I kiss goodbye any hopes of getting to the gym before Christmas. I now turn my aspirations towards accessing a good physio to expedite this alleged recovery process.

My husband and I are alone most weekends as our boys welcome the distraction of being away at school during this unexpected year. I've been the unusually stereotypical, dedicated wife this weekend not only cooking up several storms but also humouring my husband's love of rugby and Formula 1 by watching and commentating with all the sporting intellect I can muster. As we wrap up our Sunday evening, I decide to check my email and ensure all is right with my administrative world.

There it is. The email from a payment vehicle that says I've made a purchase in the United States followed by a dodgy delivery address and even dodgier said purchase. Naturally, as one does, I click on the 'I do not recognise this transaction' button. Big mistake. In fact, this is the scam within the scam. You are then taken to fake payment vehicle site which asks you to type in your email, password and then your bank sort code and card details so they can "reinstate your account". Of course, I do not oblige as, thankfully, I find this part highly questionable. This is how they access your passwords and card details. Instead, I report the email to their "spoof centre". They say they will phone me at home with a code to verify my identity.

At this very moment I get a FaceTime call. I am not a fan of FaceTime but answer thinking it's related to the aforementioned cybercrime. To my surprise, two young girls appear with long flowing manes looking vaguely bemused by my "cancer scarf" clad head. I quickly turn the camera onto the tree behind me.

I have to think fast. These girls are too young to be members of a payment vehicle site fraud team. In what seems like a flash of brilliance I conclude that they are indeed modern-day hackers. Their "cover" is to look like schoolgirls so that they can capture a 3D image of your face on FaceTime for face recognition hacking. Also, I had entered my home telephone number when following instructions so all the pieces of the puzzle are coming together. Hackers these days are very young and giggly, mind you. I gesticulate, with great fervour, at my husband to turn down the dulcet tones of *God Save our Gracious Queen* while Lewis Hamilton stands proud on the podium and find myself shouting 'darling it's the hackers!' The girls look a little dazed and confused. After asking, 'What's with the talking tree?' they disappear in a flash. Clearly, they have realised their attempted internet heist was an epic fail and evaporated into thin air.

Feeling mildly pleased with myself as newly appointed domestic cybercrime chief, I pipe back down to my admin. As we settle into the evening, one by one we get a call from the boys. I hear Jonathan easing into a conversation, but over time it becomes apparent that…well, the girls were calling our youngest son and were just quite simply, his friends hoping for a little FaceTime. Instead, they have come face to face with a mad talking tree shouting excitedly about hackers. Thank you, iCloud. I will never forget this and I have your number. My husband falls about laughing at my rendition of an "ever-so-shining Bridget Jones" moment. Even I have to relent as the incident has us both holding our sides with laughter with tears escaping down our faces. For once I will consent, I have earned the title 'chemo head'.

He texts our second-born a photo of the tree with the caption 'This is what your girlfriends think your mum looks like'. The reply comes fast and ever-wounding, 'That's quite funny, Dad. Lol'. This new gem of an incident will have us smiling for many a day. It isn't the first time and it won't be the last, but as we wander up to bed, my husband turns to me still giggling and says 'only you'. These are the moments that cancer cannot take. They are the moments that matter.

Saturday, 29 December, 2018 – The Psychology of Pain

Pain is just a four-letter word. But I will tell you that it's not only a very convincing enemy it's also what our lives are all about. Alleviating it, numbing it, living with it, or not. For me, December was all about pain. It's why it's taken me so long to write. Not so smiley a subject she says. It is the month that has proverbially caught up with me. It marks 10 months of being in pain. It marks the end of a year of pain with some glorious moments thrown in. Moments that aren't glorious if it isn't for the pain.

When you set out to run a marathon, fight a war, try and battle cancer or just get through this thing Prince called "life", you think there is a beginning, a middle and a very real end. You can't ever afford to think that the end is death (unless you are unfortunately suicidal, which is something I've never been). In September I am told, post-surgery, that in order to stay alive, I need more oral chemotherapy after my radiotherapy. From that, I move to "second line" treatment. She sighs.

Second line treatment still hasn't begun. I am told that two weeks post radiotherapy, my side effects will subside. Oh, my sweet lord do they not subside. Instead, my right reconstruction (it's a bit of a stretch to call it a breast just yet) swells up making it not only immobile but very painful to get through my exercises. After an ultrasound and blood tests, it is deemed that there is no infection or 'capsular contraction', (scar tissue build-up). But on physical examination, it becomes apparent that there is subcutaneous fluid pooling. There are a few lymph nodes, so there is no drainage. Similar to a bruised, peeling balloon building up in your body that isn't allowed to burst. Draining it by incision will only risk infection. Yes, that sepsis thing that almost killed me earlier this year. The lymphoedema (medically a dirty word for me) clinic won't touch it until eight weeks post-radio as 'draining my lymph nodes' could spread naughty, lurking cancer cells. Clever escapees. They will have escaped all the "poison, cut, burn" of the treatment stages. Trust me, they have this ability when they are triple negative.

We try and alleviate the pain via a plethora of painkillers. This doesn't help my liver she says, so I have the tendency to under medicate the amount of pain relief I need. This causes you to live with pain. Note to self: living with physical pain causes emotional pain. While this is not the first time I will cry in 10 months, the fear of death does start to creep in. The catharsis does occur. They said it would catch up with me. And catch up with me it does. I wouldn't call it a meltdown altogether, but certainly a pooling of pain. Today will be the 325th day of being in pain. I allow myself to cry and freak out, just a little. Because there is no end in sight.

If we can't alleviate it altogether, we numb it. There is an incredible plot in early Grey's Anatomy. We're only on Season two. Can I just say? McDreamy is the most splendid tool for pain numbing. If only he came in a pill. Here is a doctor to die for. Gorgeous, smart and funny with that bonus white coat. Frankly, who needs codeine? Sorry I digress. There is this plot where a train wreck has caused one singular pole to literally spear through two people. He is African American. She is Caucasian. This is not a happy accident. It's layered with metaphors. The fusion of two souls that are truly polarised. It's physically painful to watch. Yet we're told they feel no pain. Their bodies have gone in to shock. She cracks jokes as he nurtures her with words. Metaphorically speaking, I crack jokes and my husband nurtures me with words. They conclude that he stands more chances of life (having looked at scans to show pole damage) than she does. As such, they decide to pull her off the pole which will cause her to bleed to death so they can operate on him. They numb her pain of dying with anaesthesia. He lives. McDreamy cries for the first time in his career.

Living with pain is what I'm doing. My blog is called *breast-cancer-smiles* so I am choosing to see the funny side. In that context, I was in a room recently with a lot of...let's call it "earning power". I consider myself a fairly intelligent person, as intelligent people go. But here's what's not so smart. Spouting your trade to sound intelligent. Let me explain. In the same way, a poet can overwhelm by talking about iambic pentameters, so can a plumber when talking about the inner workings of a pressure pipe in a toilet. It's not clever; it's simply your trade. If anyone spent 10 hours a day for 10 years honing a discipline, they too could overwhelm you with microscopic detail. So, back to about two hours of acronyms and specialist terms and for just one moment I feel stupid. It doesn't last. I'm having relevance issues. As an ex-advertising exec, I would lose most in one second talking about ECUs and DSPs. When you eat sushi, you might notice the freshness but you won't obsess about the knife skills. As an aside, might I congratulate the producers of *Masterchef The Professionals*, because despite Greg Wallace being irritating as all hell, they have mastered a programme that is interesting to domestic cooks like me even though I won't ever come within 10 feet of a sous vide machine. People discussing their industries to outsiders can be okay if you have the "zoom out to base principles" talent. Otherwise, it is painful. My stepfather had this uncontrollable urge to lecture on the beauty of carburettors, despite not being a mechanic. As an oil man, we had to hear out the 'price of crude' often. Every time he started, it made me want to slit my wrists and let it bleed out. I jest, without straying too far from the truth. Early lessons in living with pain.

Lastly, I'll talk about "not" living with pain. Death is boring because we'll all get there in the end. But another very amusing plot in *Grey's Anatomy* is a man in spinal pain, using porn and the endorphins it releases to get rid of his pain. You read that correctly. Pornography to kill pain. I think the nugget of truth here is that positive emotions can relieve pain. At least that's how I translate it. I'll circle back to my Christmas Day this year. A gathering of family, music, food, dance and love. This definitely gets rid of the pain. My sister and her family come over. My husband cries because I'm so happy and we dance all night long like some bad Lionel Richie song. These are the things life should be made of.

I'll leave you with a thought. Why is solitary confinement in prison so painful? Because we lose physical connection. It need not be human, but any connection. Akin to the humble hug being known as a pain reducer. It's 5 am and I lie awake in bed this morning. My cat jumps up on the bed to play and after a little frolicking, she settles next to my leg. I'm trying to move my arm to a position where I feel less pain. It's by my side and she reaches out and puts her paw on my hand. I can feel her pulse and she can feel mine. This is the position I am looking for. My pain is gone for that moment. Happy New Year everyone. Whether emotional, physical or intellectual, here's to a 2019 with less pain for all.

Friday, 8 February, 2019 – One Year On: Butterfly to Chrysalis and Back

It feels like a life cycle in reverse. A butterfly morphing back into a chrysalis. To remain glass half full, I focus on the fact that a Monarch butterfly uses its brilliant orange colour to ward off predators. Orange signifies they are toxic to eat. Each winter, their journey lasts thousands of miles as their eyes track the sun's position in the sky to guide them to their destination. This journey takes six generations because of this species' short life span. But what a life. Imagine reverting to a chrysalis and restarting that journey. It's a rebirth not many want, but a rebirth all the same.

It is -2 as I play tennis that day. The lump is burgeoning. A lump that is the beginning of an end to the woman that stands on that tennis court. That day she is smashing forehands down the line. As of now, she has limited use of her right arm. Let's rephrase that. This is the day I have sashayed into the world of breast cancer.

Fast forward one year to February 8, 2019. What a year. What a world. One in which my understanding of pain has deepened as has my connection with the human race. A time that has enabled a stronger self, a person I had no idea existed. The truth is, I will never be without cancer again. Whether full-blown and ready to fly as it was in my lymph nodes, microscopic and undetectable through modern technology as it might be now or just marinating in my head for the future. I simply can't exist without it.

'Isn't she supposed to be making us smile?' I hear you say. Yes, but only after I've indulged in my very small, inner self-pity squeak. Squeak over.

In January 2019, between treatments, I fly to Nashville in the US to visit my mother in her new home. I have handled my pre-flight jitters with a visit to my oncologist who assures me that as long as I stay hydrated, this ballooning chest (post-op/post-radio oedema) will not explode. A good movie and a dehydrating glass of special juice are exactly what the doctor ordered. I flatten my bed and settle into a deep, pressurised slumber. Triumph is amok as I waltz off the flight, self-congratulating. I have made it without literally exploding into a thousand pieces (the brain is a powerful organ). I'm immediately accosted by the charming local tone of hospitality during an endless walk below seven billboards. They all say 'Welcome Y'all' in a different language. The "Welcome" is translated. The "Y'all" is not.

Feeling very, very welcome, I enter US immigration with the usual *My Name is Khan* expectations. I'm pleasantly surprised by a delightful, aged gentleman who goes down his list and finally asks if I've 'got ny druugs'.

'Yes', I say, clutching my controlled substances like my life depends on it. I tell him my oncologist has prescribed them and that I have a letter stating permission to carry them.

'Your oncle gave you druugs gurl?'

Correction, 'No not my uncle, my O-n-c-o-l-o-g-i-s-t.'

And with that, I'm free to find my mum and all the culinary delights that I know awaits me in her new home.

I get talking to my cousin that evening, who uncovers the world of "smoking". Not cigarettes but smoking meat or at least that's my impression. It's a cultural delicacy in Nashville. This is a science whittled down to a fine art if there is such a thing. It involves temperature probes, marinade injections, hand-built barbecue pits highly tempered cooking rubs and smoking techniques. As a person fascinated with the world of cuisine, I'm had. I say yes to a "pit" party the following day. Hell yeah, I'm all things chicken wings.

Give this little episode your best attention as it is a snapshot of life on a different planet, geographically, politically, emotionally and intellectually. It's pouring that day, so the mind boggles at how I'm going to attend a barbecue. Undercover, I'm told. Not in detective gear mind, but in a garage. Somewhere we will be able to see and smell the pit but not get assaulted by rain. Makes perfect sense.

Howdy folks, let me transport you to a destination garage in the middle of some woods in Nashville. I'm told it's full of voters on the "other side". I vow not to open my political mouth as there could be guns, liquor and ammo involved. This "garage" is not your typical garage. Cars are not housed here. This is fully equipped with a homemade bar, a 55" TV, a deep freeze (which I'm praying doesn't have formaldehyde-soaked Democrats in it), a 6' mastiff called Minnie (as in Mouse), a tonne of Heineken and 25 cigarettes worth of smoke. I've missed out the nine people that look at me with a 'wtf is that?' expression. This is a smoking garage in Tennessee when pit weather fails. All six feet of Minnie and I are becoming friends.

As my eyes redden and bulge with passive smoke penetration, I'm thinking, *Right. If the breast cancer doesn't get me, lung cancer's on its way.* So, ice is there for the breaking and being the extrovert, I decide it needs a sledgehammer. I have a lady puffing up a storm asking how long my flight was. I talk of some nine hours spent in the air. Cut to guy with white goatee 'Ain't no 'f*!?ing way I'd spend nan hires in no plane.' The lady agrees. She is my age with three grandchildren in their teens. I'm feeling a little behind on the life goals.

Digging to the bottom of my social resources, I find some common ground in one of my favourite films *Fried Green Tomatoes*. A Kathy Bates classic. I proceed to do the thing that I do quite well. My litany of accent impersonations. This strikes a chord. Feeling very pleased with myself, I rattle off the lines 'Boy you gotta good scald on that chicken dear'. Laughter. This seems to have achieved the social lubrication required.

My eyes dart across the room as my cousin's baby arrives. He's restricted to the warm smoke-free kitchen. I leap towards said baby with the desire to be his newfound mother in need of solitary confinement. In this kitchen, in the woods, in

Tennessee, I hap across a delightful British girl and her boyfriend. He is about to tour Europe having been in some famous folk band which has escaped me. It's my bad because even my husband knows the band. This makes them huge potatoes because he knows no bands. Ever. We exchange life stories and Instagram followings. Who knew?

My cousin's smoked brisket is second to none. His Himalayan salt-rubbed baked potatoes equally good. He bolts into the room proclaiming, 'They luurve you!' I smile feeling genuinely pleased with myself. He makes me do a pinkie promise that we will never argue because of political opinion again. I agree. He's a sweet soul made even sweeter by the fact that when he picks up his phone he greets with 'Yellow!' It makes me giggle every time.

Our friendship is the result of familial history and failure of the 'divide and conquer' rule adopted by a certain leader who shall remain nameless. These are unions you can't make up, but they are unions all the same. I do learn one thing. That even people we think we can't relate to, living different lives, valuing polar opposite ideals, can find grounds to share – the need to eat, laugh and exist. Okay, our need to breathe oxygen may differ but small differences are healthy. Armageddon has been averted.

'She's gone mad', I hear you say. 'We wanted her to make us laugh not mess with our emotional foundations.' It's a beautifully finished trip with my brother arriving together with his wife and two children. We spend around 48 hours alone laughing until we cry. Can I just say? His kids make my kids look like axe murderers. Or is it that they are eight, six, and very sweet. Mine are 16 and 14. Hmmm. The jury is out on that one. I jest. Boys, if you're reading this, Mama loves you dearly. I can assure you they have high tailed it from where ever they are and are reading no more.

It is an important story and forays into new life and new meaning, you understand. Before I take you back to the chrysalis, I want to thank you for sharing my journey, for all the feedback, love and hundreds of messages I've received about my writing. I hope you'll stay with me.

As I start another year and another round of chemotherapy this week, I will need to begin again. The oral chemo will last until June. Then treatment is over but progresses to cosmetic surgery later in the year. I'm praying I don't lose my hair. I'm praying that this will work. I'm praying I'm not too different a butterfly. I'm praying I can pinpoint the sun and get to my destination. This has been a new formation, in a different body, with a different mind in a similar shell. For now, I'm flying on a wing and a prayer, but I'm still flying.

Wednesday, 27 February, 2019 – The 'F' Word

This is the title of an email in my inbox. Doubling up as an expletive, it is actually an enquiry from a rightly concerned parent asking for advice and tips on this "festival fad" among teenagers. To be honest that horse has bolted and this ship sailed. What is a parent today supposed to do with this alleged alcohol, drug-fuelled, questionable music fest that is the "F" word? From where I'm sitting; "F" is for Festival. "C" is for Cancer. "P" is for Perspective.

"F" is for Festival
I hark back to the day when festivals were symbols of freedom, part of sartorial and musical expression with

occasional philanthropic overtures thrown in. I can feel your face flush and sigh as you read. Imagery is loaded with psychedelic colours, VW symbols and peace motifs. For the most part, there were concerts where singalongs were common and flames lit the world instead of iPhones. Then, there was Live Aid. "Cute popstars" crooned together clutching their headsets while emotionally belting out to proper composition. And everybody wanted to "Feed the World". Adorable.

I exaggerate but cut to the present day. Think washed-up supermodels trudging through muddy puddles in their designer wellies, clad in vomit-soaked mini skorts-trying to look like newbies smoking doobies. Speakers blaring mindless chatter to backbeats that were music once. This, while "G's" gather around campsites cultivating their rapster accents worshipping the guy who's always stoned – because that's apparently dope. Fast forward 10 years to guy lolling around in a bobbly, unwashed dressing gown smelling like mould, smoking said spliff, jobless and slurring. It's called 'brain turned to mush or writing on the wall' syndrome.

Spoiler alert detected. To wave a small but not inconsequential marijuana peace flag (if there is such a thing) I'm not all things anti-cannabis then. Rumour has it that CBD oil is the best analgesic going. Apparently, it's pain relief for the kings of rugby. Only when its batch tested and from the right source says my pain doctor who's involved in a pain relief study with cannabis oil. So toke that!

However, don't get me started on this tooty-fruity-vaping nonsense. A perfect training tool to get your kid smoking even if they never intended it. Why? Because you start with watermelon-flavoured nicotine until they're so addicted, they're past caring. Hence, the graduation to cigarettes. Genius. At least it's tobacco company brilliance. Only now, you also smell like a boot soaked in an ashtray. As I say to my son, imagine the scientific evidence required to get a company to write on their own packaging that their product kills you. If the "Smoking Kills" packaging fails, they can always turn to the phenomenon I call natural selection.

"C" is for Cancer.

I live in a world where I'm trying to get my right arm above my head. My dreams of playing tennis sit in a remote corner of my brain, whilst surviving the next year occupies most of it. My surgeries at the end of the year loom so I can start rehab all over again. My skin from radiotherapy burns and is still shedding. It's the darkest tan I've ever had. My chemo tablets are making me sick as a dog. But half term still consists of driving my eldest to recording studios in North London whilst chewing on spearmint gum like a nutter to stop me puking brown toast over an unsuspecting steering wheel.

I marvel at the irony here. While some fantasise over their various artists following and YouTube views, I listen to a pharmacist in a private room giving me a 15-minute lecture on how to handle my chemo tablets. These are no ordinary tablets. They are ones I have to take with momentary precision. I have to eat a full meal at 8 am (the thought of which makes me hurl), take three tablets within half an hour, wash my hands and repeat every 12 hours for two weeks with one week off over five months. The irony is that I'm to rinse so much as a hint of tablet residue off my hands lest it come into remote contact with other living beings. Yet it's okay for me to ingest six whole tablets in one day. All this for 8% increased survival. This precious little factoid is waning my interest in festivals.

"P" is for Perspective.

'Back to the lecture at hand' in the famous words of Dr Dre (*Nuthin' but a G thang*). Just call me old school trendy. I have a lot of proverbial rotten fish to fry, but that doesn't mean I've washed my hands of my children. Oh, no. I have stood at matches in the pouring rain freezing my radiotherapy-pummelled extremities off. I have hobbled around the house packing their bags with one working arm because my lymph nodes have been gouged out. I have made fresh stock with homemade gyozas for the sweet cherubs to devour whilst feeling chemo-sick. But we still live in the world of obsessive parenting where gratitude is just a very, long word. At the end of the day, I will always sport a long, crooked nose, wear a tall, pointy, black cloak resplendent with hood whilst "pimping my ride" on a very long broomstick.

In between numerous cancer engagements I have sewn myself quite the new career – the business of curing my cancer and raising awareness in a culture that seems to have a Master's degree in denial. But I'm increasingly perplexed at the "festival" question. I am fully aware my kids will attend them. Short of sitting on their heads and micromanaging their every move, perhaps I do have some options. I could hold all UK-based drug barons hostage until my child is safely indoors. Please WhatsApp me for tickets to that show. I can make the word 'hostage' sound really sexy. I could have a Wi-Fi connected camera installed in my son's forehead telling him he is a Mission Impossible agent or I could handcuff him to the front door dressed as a policewoman. Though that might be a slightly more effective reprimand for my husband. Failing which, there is always the naughty step.

Barring all of the above, we are taking the view that my eldest is going to be 18 in the not too distant future. We are going to have to rely on our parenting to date balanced with his reasonable rites of passage. I say reasonable because this is our home which they must respect, including the freedoms we enable. Tell that to the teenage brain. However, what the teenage brain should understand is, they don't yet earn the multi-coloured notes. Hopefully, we all have children with a broader language and understanding of the world than that. All I understand is my plight to stay alive. In that context, I think I'm going to have to embellish the "F" word with "NFI". It stands for Not Festival Interested.

Wednesday, 6 March, 2019 – Mastectomy. The Sum of All Fears

I read this article three days before my surgery. I thought long and hard about cancelling. I'm glad my husband talked me out of it because I would most likely be dead by now.

Journalism can be thought-provoking. It can push boundaries. It can also take an opinionated slant or tell the story of a biopic, singular experience. What it shouldn't do, is undermine any singular truth. When I first read this eye-grabbing headline, I did a double-take. In basic summary, it's the story of a woman with invasive breast cancer who decides last minute, a mastectomy isn't for her. Apparently, her breasts are too psychologically and physically important to go through with it and what's more, it might be unnecessary. She cancels her surgery, has a lumpectomy, radiotherapy, keeps her breasts intact, is still alive and Bob's your Uncle. While I'm utterly delighted this journalist has held on to her body parts, many of us do not have that liberty. The perfect analogy is a "No-Deal Brexit". It puts us in recession, come life or death. I qualified as a journalist too, but I think long and hard about my opinionated musings on a blog, let alone a broadsheet with the readership of millions. However, I thank this article for teaching me one thing. As a woman, I refuse to be defined by my body parts. My message is you are far more than the sum of those parts.

Intentions may have been good. The outcome leads us to question the medical necessity for this surgery. Agreed. It may have been an automated choice for years, even a seemingly preventative one. I can't argue medically whether this surgery was necessary or not. But what if it is deemed necessary? What about all the women that don't have the luxury of preserving their alleged self-esteems and body image? How does this article make them feel? Sure, we should ask the question but at the same time understand this surgery is sometimes absolutely necessary. Let me dare to address our inherent Page-3-meets-Madonna psyche. One of the very stigmas my blog attempts to question. Here are just some of the quotes that left giant-sized exclamations in my head. Think, wide-eyed emoji.

"My breasts seemed such an important part of me. I'd breastfed each of my four children for three years."
(The Guardian Article 'Cancer I could deal with, losing my breast I could not' - Joanna Moorhead)

Excellent. Mammary gland purpose served. Or as Gordon Ramsey would say 'Milking done'. Personally, I was never able to breastfeed and tortured myself for weeks after childbirth feeling like a terrible mother, under-nourishing my innocent babies. Both times, I tried and I cried. My expressing yielded 1ml of dishwater-like fluid in an hour. This, with an electric milking machine that would have dried up most cows. If it tasted good, my son did not let on. Eventually, my inner Madonna took a hike. I switched to a hypoallergenic formula which might as well have been Wagyu beef consommé for its price. My sons lapped it up like cats that got the cream and still quite like me (to answer any bonding queries). As far as their health is concerned, touch wood, they give Dwayne "The Rock" Johnson a run for his money. I jest. Breast may be best, but if not, your best is good enough.

"I've always loved my breasts. They're an important part of my sexuality, as essential to my sense of myself in their way as my heart or my lungs."

(The Guardian Article 'Cancer I could deal with, losing my breast I could not' - Joanna Moorhead)

Alrighty then. Where shall I begin? First, congratulations on the self-love. This is a quest I'm still grappling with. Though this smack of Bridget Jones' view of "smug-marrieds". Second, why have two mammary glands hanging from one's chest been elevated to objects of desire and titillation? Okay, I'll stop fighting that battle. No point questioning caveman mentality now. True. They are a part of most women's sexuality I suppose. Including those women that have to have a mastectomy. "Desperately seeking" sensitivity chip. Excuse the Madonna analogies today. Third, likening breasts to your heart or your lungs. Really? Because I'm still kicking around *without* one of my original breasts. Yet, the old heart is still beating and lungs still breathing. Anyone who wants to try either of those activities without a transplant, step forward into the noose, please.

"My big fear was that I'd be diminished by a mastectomy, that I'd never again feel whole, or truly confident or comfortable with myself."

(The Guardian Article 'Cancer I could deal with, losing my breast I could not' - Joanna Moorhead)

And there we have it. The sum of all fears. Yes, all these fears are real, even realised. But what about the women that have to live with this? How is this article helping them navigate the difficulty this person is lucky enough to have circumvented? I won't posture as the end result. But I'm on a good road, whereby I may just feel a different kind of whole. Oh, and I might live to tell the tale.

"In case I'm sounding brave, let me confess; I'm absolutely not."

(The Guardian Article 'Cancer I could deal with, losing my breast I could not' - Joanna Moorhead)

"Brave" did not come to mind. Someone running for the hills maybe. It might be the road less travelled but the self-love is feeling a little skin deep here. However, it is a personal choice that we must respect. Just to give a glimpse of the other side. I was told by the lymphoedema clinic that I needed more support and was shown one of the ugliest contraptions I have ever considered putting on my body. In search of said "bra", I came across a range in M&S that ticked those boxes I never wanted to tick but grateful that they had thought about post-surgery. 'It's just until you're better' says my reassuring other half. He has these amazing lenses. They're the 'you look amazing no matter what' lenses. More husbands need to have them. With the said item in hand, I wait in the queue only to hear the bellowing voice of the cashier, 'You do know those are post-surgical bras, don't you?'

I think, *No love, I thought I was in Agent Provocateur buying a mesh thong set with tassels.* I say, 'Yes, thank you.' I get tea and sympathy looks from the queue. As John Wainwright once said, 'There is no such thing as bravery; only degrees of fear.'

"Breast cancer, after all, won't kill me: the bigger danger is of the original cancer returning in another part of my body, and that danger wasn't affected by my decision not to have a mastectomy."

I'm not medically qualified, but having checked this article with an oncologist, it appears littered with inconsistencies and errors. I'm assuming the fact-checker and editor at the said newspaper had gone on a long sabbatical, taken a holiday or flown over the cuckoo's nest when allowing this little piece to fly out the door. I have it on good authority that breast cancer can indeed kill you.

Now that I got that off my metaphoric chest, I leave you with a quote from a movie that I think holds true to one's duty as a journalist.

"**You're about to breathe air that's way over your pay grade so listen up. You're going to be asked for analysis and advice, so be God damn sure you know what you're talking about before you give it. Don't be afraid to say you don't know. Choose your words carefully, words have a habit of being turned into policy.**"

Cabot. A Sum of All Fears.

Epilogue

'Creed' – Winning in the Ring Against Cancer

How do you win in the ring with cancer? There's a final fight in the movie, Creed. His opponent is Victor Drago, a stunning metaphor for terminal disease. This is a fight Creed chooses. It is not one I chose. He only sees winning if Drago loses. I do not see victory singularly this way. Most cancer patients' only definition of triumph is staying alive. Mine isn't. I see a greyer realm of possibilities of how you win in the ring against cancer.

Every time I get a knock-out punch, I see this final fight scene in slow motion. The punch, the face turn, the blood and fluid flying through the air. Slow, until he hits the floor and his life flashes before him. Everyone is shouting for him to get up, his inner voice is pleading the same. His body is telling him to stop. But get up he does. He does this, because he wants to win. So do I. I just have a different definition.

Here's what cancer doesn't have to take. You. The 'you' people know and love, the 'you' people will remember. My worst fear is to leave morphed into the hysterical scream, pain and fear of a cancer patient. Like at the end of a play when the last scene dies out and all you see is smoke from dry ice and echoes of silence where sounds of life were once so dramatically present. This is when the cancer has won.

My first response to cancer is to say it won't have all of me. My second response has been that I find it hard to cause pain by sharing mine. Let's talk about my third. The last unorthodox element is that I am not afraid of death. This sounds morbid, ridiculous and untrue. To sum it up succinctly, my first 25 years weren't a great debut. I was very unhappy until I met my soulmate in my late 20's. With counselling, his love, guidance and friendship, I found peace and forgiveness. I am being honest when I say, I wouldn't exchange these last 20 years with anyone else's 80. Of course, life had its ups and downs. But if I say I'm not afraid of death, it's because I've felt so loved, not because I haven't.

To those who think my smiles are insincere or strange, that's one's prerogative. I couldn't have predicted this response prior to cancer. My reaction has been as natural as breathing, but to the universe something of an oddity. 'Breast-cancer-smiles' is after all a contradiction in terms. Stranger than fiction, I wrote my irony-drenched ethos for living a long time ago.

"Lives hard, loves hard, plays hard. I'd rather have 50 full years than 100 empty ones."

I can only suppose someone was listening. I hope to turn 50 on March 26th, 2021.

My body is one part of me, my soul is another. Cancer will most likely take my body at some point. It will never have my soul. And that is how I will beat cancer and win. Dead, or alive.

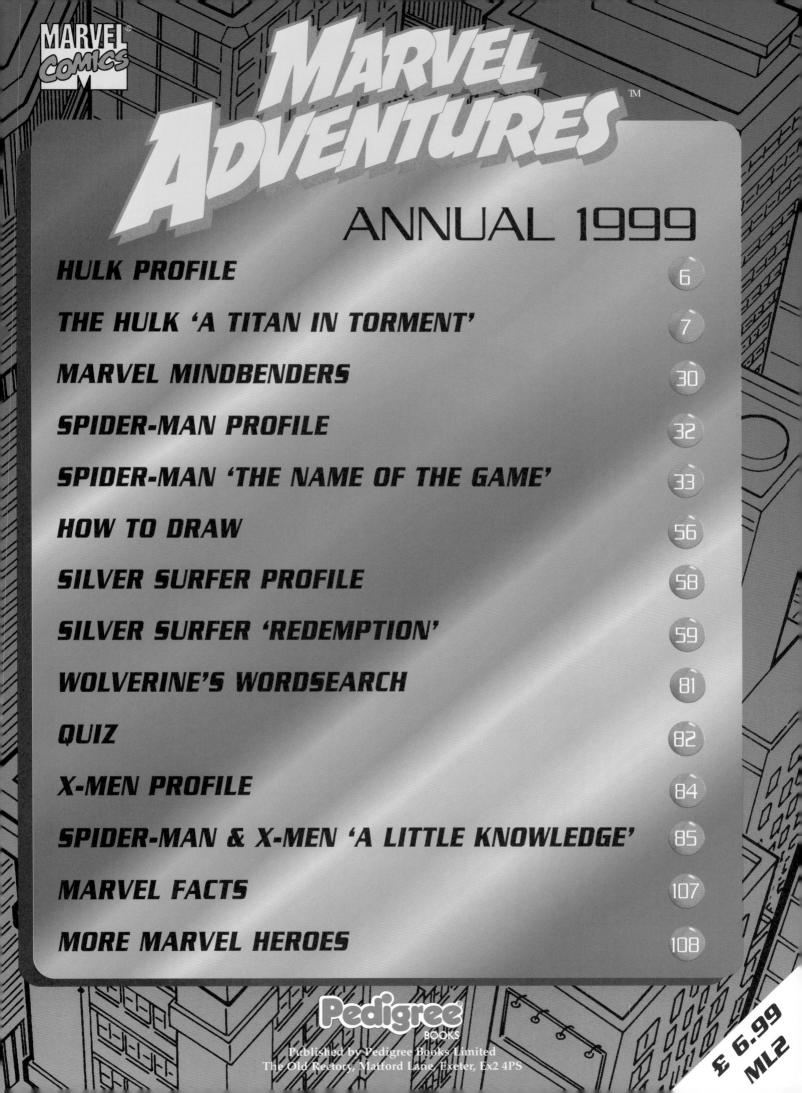

MARVEL COMICS

MARVEL ADVENTURES™

ANNUAL 1999

Pedigree BOOKS

Published by Pedigree Books Limited
The Old Rectory, Matford Lane, Exeter, Ex2 4PS

£ 6.99

ML2

THE INCREDIBLE HULK

Profile: The Incredible Hulk

Scientist Dr. Bruce Banner designed the highly destructive 'gamma bomb' whilst working in a U.S. government nuclear research facility. During the first detonation of his device, Banner was irradiated with highly-charged radioactive particles. Due to an unknown genetic factor in his body, he was not killed by the radiation...but he was never the same again.

From that day on, whenever he became angry, the release of adrenaline would transform Banner into a powerful, green-skinned monster. Bestial, nearly mindless and possessing the strength of two hundred men, The Hulk was soon feared by everyone - including Banner himself.

- *Real name:* Robert Bruce Banner
- *Occupation:* Nuclear physicist
- *Base of operations:* New Mexico
- *Abilities:* Possesses high degree of resistance to injury, pain and disease. His superhuman strength enables him to lift in excess of 100 tons.
- *Weapon:* None
- *Height:* 7 ft.
- *Weight:* 1040 lbs
- *Eyes:* Green
- *Hair:* Dark green
- *Skin:* Green

Now read on to see The Hulk star in our first titanic tale!

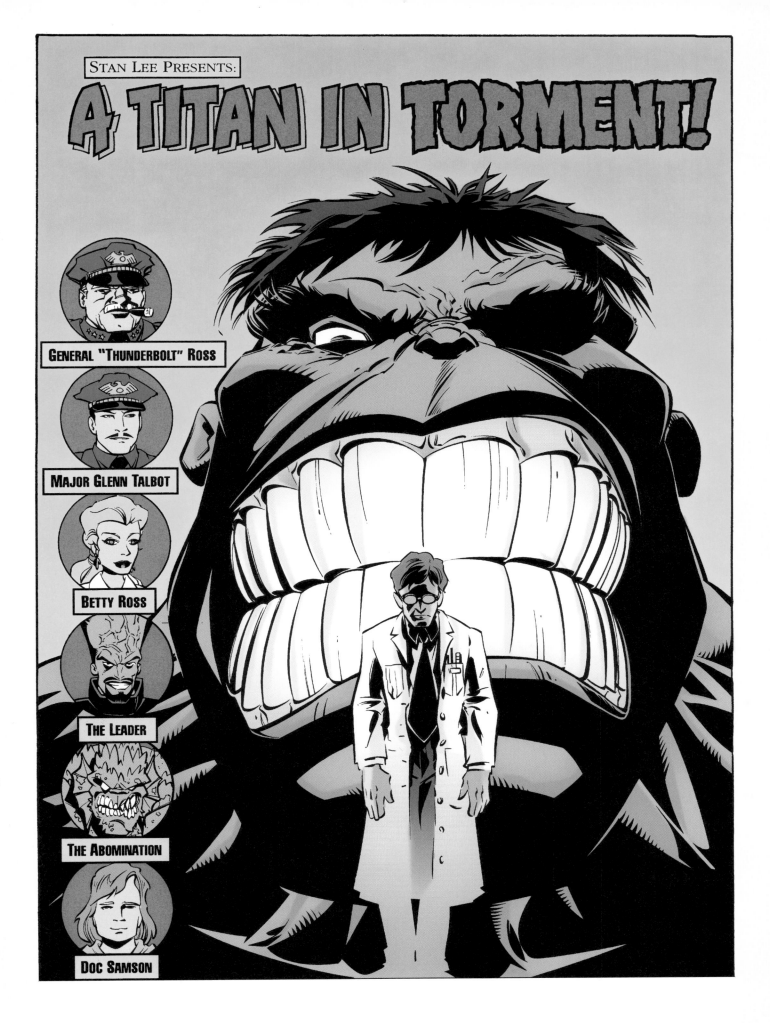

ON A DARE I DROVE MY JALOPY OUT ONTO THE TEST SITE OF THE NEW *GAMMA RAY BOMB.*

"*Dr. ROBERT BRUCE BANNER*-- CREATOR OF THE BOMB-- SAW ME FROM THE CONTROL BUNKER.

"HE *RISKED* HIS LIFE TO *SAVE* ME-- SHOVING ME INTO A PIT BEFORE THE BOMB WAS DETONATED.

"HE WASN'T SO *LUCKY.* BANNER WAS *CAUGHT* IN THE BLAST--

"--AND *TRANSFORMED* INTO THAT THING BEHIND THE WALL...

"...THAT *INCREDIBLE HULK!*"

ON THE OTHER SIDE OF THAT MASSIVE BLOCK, A BIZARRE TRANSFORMATION IS OCCURRING...

I-- IT'S *OVER* FOR NOW. ONCE AGAIN, I'M CHANGING FROM THE HULK *BACK* INTO BRUCE BANNER.

RICK-- IT'S ME, BRUCE. YOU CAN OPEN THE DOOR-- THE MONSTER'S *GONE*... FOR NOW.

I *HEAR* YOU.

RRRRRR

MY GOD-- IT WAS *WORSE* THIS TIME, RICK! ONCE I FELT THE CHANGE COMING OVER ME--

--MY INTELLIGENCE *RECEDING* INTO THE BRUTE... I WASN'T SURE I'D *EVER* TURN BACK INTO A MAN..

I'VE *GOT* TO FIND SOME WAY OUT-- SOME *CURE.* Ohh... LEGS WEAK-- FEEL SHAKY. RICK-- Help....

DON'T WORRY, BRUCE. I'VE *GOT* YOU. I'LL BE *WITH* YOU UNTIL YOU'VE GOT THIS *LICKED!*

I'M YOUR *FRIEND,* REMEMBER THAT!

MILES AWAY, THERE EXISTS A HIGH-TECH FACILITY WHICH WAS BUILT *SPECIFICALLY* TO DEAL WITH THE THREAT POSED BY THE GREEN GOLIATH--

--HULKBUSTER BASE!

INSIDE THE COMPOUND, SOLDIERS WEARING SUITS OF OMNIUM STEEL-MESH ARMOR HONE THEIR BATTLE PROWESS AGAINST HOLOGRAMS OF THE HULK.

THEY'RE DOING SUPERBLY, *MAJOR TALBOT.*

THANK YOU, SIR.

BETTY, MAJOR TALBOT HERE PUT THIS UNIT TOGETHER AND HE'S DONE A *FANTASTIC* JOB!

HE'S THE KIND OF MAN YOU SHOULD BE SPENDING *TIME* WITH-- RATHER THAN THAT MILKSOP TURNED MENACE, *BRUCE BANNER!*

DAD, PLEASE.

OH, BRUCE... IF ONLY THIS HORRIBLE THING HADN'T HAPPENED TO YOU!

IT'S ALMOST MORE THAN I CAN *BEAR*-- WATCHING THEM PREPARE TO *DESTROY* YOU! I'D GIVE *ANYTHING* TO HAVE YOU COME BACK TO ME!

THOOM

WHAT IN *BLAZES* WAS THAT?

11

HULKBUSTER BASE...

MAJOR TALBOT, AS SOON AS I CAN SEPARATE BETTY FROM THE HULK, I'M GOING TO *ANNIHILATE* THAT *OBSCENITY* OF NATURE!

ALL THE MILITARY MIGHT AT MY *COMMAND* WILL BE BROUGHT TO BEAR TO BRING ABOUT THAT MONSTER'S *DESTRUCTION!*

GENERAL, PERHAPS WE COULD *CAPTURE* THE HULK-- USE GAS GRENADES TO STUN HIM, THEN *RETURN* HIM HERE FOR STUDY.

STUDY?! THIS *ISN'T* A RESEARCH OUTPOST, MAJOR! THIS BASE EXISTS FOR ONLY *ONE* PURPOSE...

GENERAL ROSS

...TO *DESTROY* THAT GREENSKINNED MONSTROSITY *BEFORE* HE KILLS A SINGLE HUMAN BEING!

DO I MAKE MYSELF *CLEAR?*

GENERAL ROSS! I'VE GOTTA SPEAK TO YOU RIGHT *NOW!*

≷Hrruummphh!≷ WHAT'S THE *MEANING* OF THIS OUT-BURST?

YOU'RE THAT BLASTED *TEENAGER*--RICK JONES --THAT BANNER THREW IN THE PIT BEFORE THE GAMMA BOMB WENT OFF!

WHAT DO YOU *WANT* HERE?

I *HAD* TO SEE YOU, SIR. BRUCE BANNER'S IN A *HORRIBLE* STATE OF MIND! HE'S BEING TORN *APART* BY THOSE CONSTANT CHANGES INTO THE HULK!

I TRY TO KEEP HIM BEHIND THE *GRANITE DOOR* IN THE CAVE WHEN HE BECOMES THAT *THING,* BUT IT MAY NOT HOLD OUT *FOREVER!*

IF YOU PROMISE TO *HELP* HIM, I'M SURE HE'D TURN HIMSELF IN.

YOU SAID *CAVE,* BOY. THERE ARE ONLY A FEW WE'VE MAPPED IN *THIS* AREA. SO *THAT'S* WHERE HE'S HOLED UP!

WH-- WHAT'RE YOU GONNA DO?

WHAT I'VE WANTED TO DO SINCE THIS NIGHTMARE *BEGAN!*

NOW YOU JUST STAY OUT OF THE WAY, SON.

16

SUDDENLY...

AWAY WITH YOU! THERE WILL BE NO FURTHER *HARM* DONE TO THIS POOR CREATURE WHILE *THE ABOMINATION* LIVES!

I AM YOUR *ONLY* FRIEND, RAMPAGING ONE. I HAVE COME TO *HELP* YOU.

HELP HULK?

WE MUST LEAVE *NOW* BEFORE REINFORCEMENTS ARE SENT IN!

T H O K

I *KNOW* WHERE *BETTY ROSS* IS. I WILL *TAKE* YOU TO HER. I AM SOMEONE YOU CAN *TRUST.*

YOU HELP HULK, SO HULK WILL GO WITH YOU.

22

HOLD YOUR FIRE, MEN! WE'LL TRACK THEM DOWN BY MEANS OF INFRA-RED SIGNATURE!

HURTING HEAD WILL *NOT* STOP HULK FROM *DESTROYING* THE ONES WHO LIED TO HIM!

NOTHING WILL STOP HULK!

SHOOM

YOU *CANNOT* BEAT HULK! BECAUSE THE *MADDER* HULK GETS, THE *STRONGER* HULK GETS!

I'LL RETREAT TO A SAFER PART OF THE COMPOUND AND DEAL WITH THE SURVIVOR LATER... WHEN HE IS IN A WEAKENED STATE FROM HIS EXERTIONS.

I AM THE ONE WHO CANNOT BE DEFEATED, FOOL-- FOR I WAS GIVEN AN EVEN *MORE* MASSIVE DOSE OF GAMMA RADIATION--

--THAN YOU RECEIVED FROM THE GAMMA BOMB EXPLOSION!

I AM--*ARRRHHH!*

PAIN-- INSIDE-- SO INTENSE-- FEEL AS IF I'M *BURNING UP!*

WHY YOU *STOP* FIGHTING? HULK *NOT* HIT YOU *THAT* HARD YET!

27

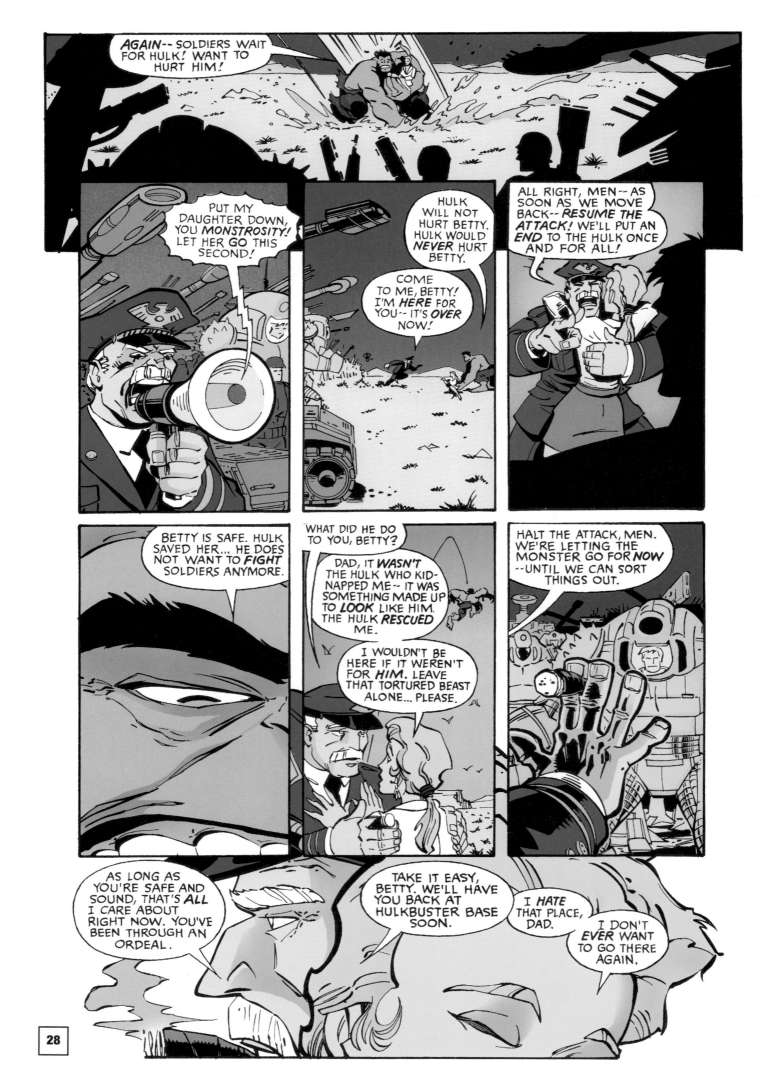

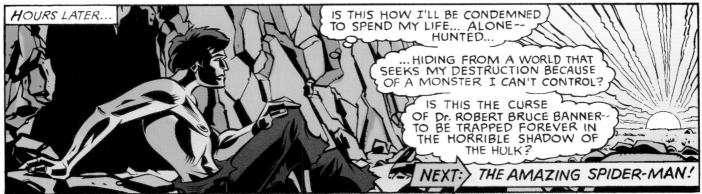

NEXT: *THE AMAZING SPIDER-MAN!*

Mighty Marvel Mindbenders!

Time for a few brainteasers to keep you on your toes! You'll find the answers at the bottom of the page - as if you need them!

DARK FORCES

You think you know your Marvel superheroes? See if you can identify these four by their silhouettes alone!

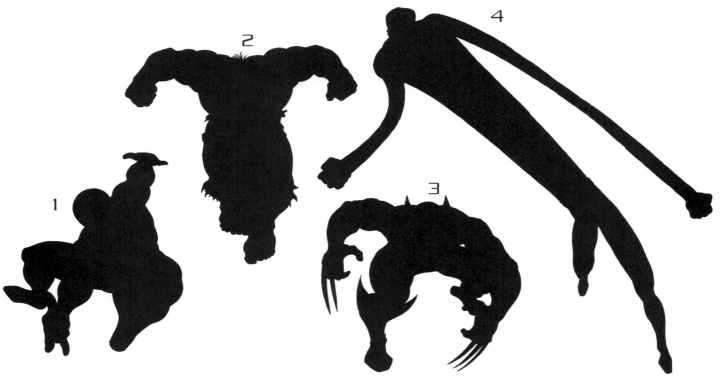

SUPERHEROINES

Unjumble these letters to find the names of six formidable Marvel females.

1. TROMS
2. HEKSULH
3. IVANMONIBLISEW
4. SAJONDER
5. DREAMPOWSNI
6. NAJEEGYR

PARAPHERNALIA
To which superheroes do each of these things belong?

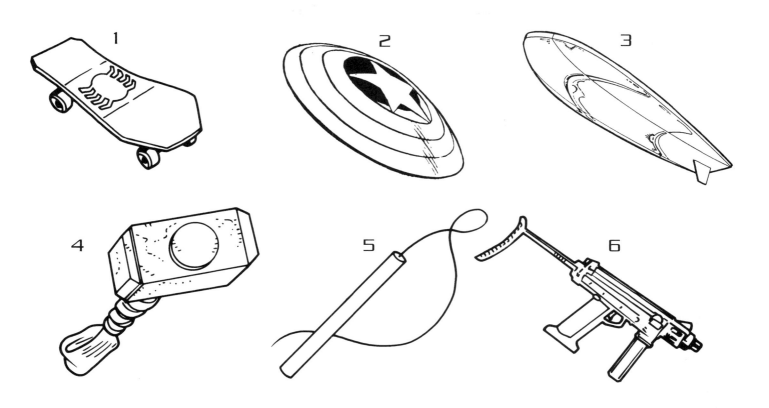

THE WAY TO H.Q.

**Reed Richards has called a meeting for the Fantastic Four.
Show Johnny Storm the quickest way to Four Freedoms Plaza.**

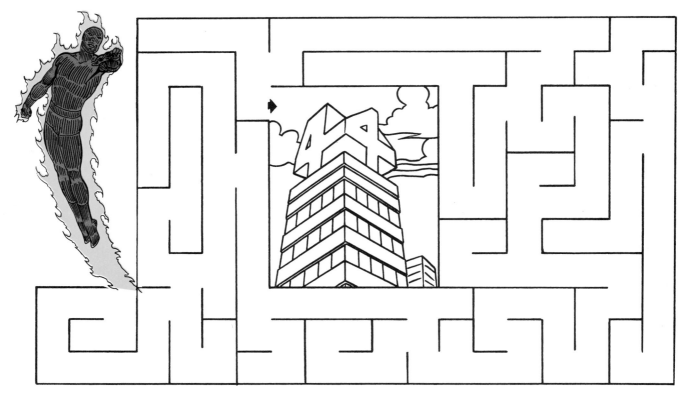

Profile: The Amazing Spider-Man

Peter Parker was just an ordinary student until the day he attended a science exhibition and his world was turned upside down. During a demonstration on the safe handling of nuclear waste, a common house spider crawled into the path of a particle accelerators beam and was massively irradiated. The stricken spider fell on Peter's hand, bit him and died. The rest, as they say, is history.

Suddenly, Peter found he could stick to walls and climb sheer surfaces; he could bend steel bars and sense unseen dangers. He created his famous red and blue costume and a fantastic device capable of weaving super-strong webs, and thus became The Amazing Spider-Man.

- **Real name:** Peter Parker
- **Occupation:** Freelance photographer, adventurer, graduate student
- **Base of operations:** New York City
- **Abilities:** Possesses superhuman strength, reflexes and equilibrium; sticks to most surfaces; has a subconscious promonitional 'danger' sense.
- **Weapon:** Web shooters (twin devices worn on wrists, which shoot a tough, flexible fibre with extraordinary adhesive properties).
- **Height:** 5 ft 10 ins.
- **Weight:** 165 lbs.
- **Eyes:** Hazel
- **Hair:** Brown

Read on to see Spidey in action against a foe with a sting in his tail!

35

A SEEDY HOTEL ON MANHATTAN'S LOWER EAST SIDE...

...WHERE EDDIE BROCK, FUGITIVE FROM JUSTICE, HIDES OUT.

SO JAMESON'S STILL *OBSESSED* WITH SPIDER-MAN... BLAMING HIM FOR *EVERY* CRIME IN THE CITY.

WELL, I'VE GOT NO LOVE FOR *EITHER* OF THEM.

I WAS *FIRED* AS A REPORTER FROM THE BUGLE BECAUSE THE WEB-SPINNER PUT THE *LIE* TO AN EXPOSÉ I WAS WRITING.

I WAS *OSTRACIZED* BY MY OWN KIND-- AND TURNED TO *CRIME* TO SURVIVE.

SPIDER-MAN & SCORPION IN CAHOOTS!
CITIZENS IMPERILED: An EDITORIAL by J.JONAH JAMESON

BUT I'LL HAVE MY *REVENGE!*

I'M GOING *AFTER* "FEARLESS" JONAH. AND WHEN I FINISH WITH *THAT* SNAKE, THE WALL-CRAWLING *FREAK* WHO WRECKED MY CAREER IS *NEXT!*

EDDIE BROCK IS NOT A MAN TO BE DISMISSED. NO WAY.

37

I HAVE TO LOOK AROUND THE CORNER --SEE IF ANYONE'S THERE.

LOOKS LIKE SOME HALF-DRESSED *BUM.* SO *THAT'S* IT.

WHAT'S THE *MEANING* OF THIS? I DON'T LIKE BEING *STALKED* FOR SPARE CHANGE.

DO YOU *KNOW* WHO I *AM,* MY GOOD MAN?

OH, I KNOW *EXACTLY* WHO YOU ARE.

YOU--*BROCK!* STAY BACK OR I'LL CALL THE POLICE!

YOU'RE GOING TO DO *NOTHING,* JAMESON. YOU'RE A *WEASEL* AND YOU'VE ALWAYS BEEN ONE.

I WAS A DEDICATED REPORTER FOR THE BUGLE AND YOU *FIRED* ME FOR *ONE* STUPID *MISTAKE.*

WELL, THAT'S GONNA *COST* YOU, JONAH. COST YOU *BIG TIME.*

D-DON'T YOU THREATEN ME, BROCK...

Yeah. I'M REAL SCARED.

YOU HAVEN'T HEARD THE LAST OF THIS-- NOT BY A LONGSHOT.

40

THE FOLLOWING DAY, NEW YORK'S EVER-AMAZING ARACHNID SWINGS INTO ACTION...

NOW GENTS, YOU SHOULD KNOW THAT WEARING *SKI MASKS* IN THE MIDDLE OF *MAY* WAS A DEAD GIVEAWAY THAT YOU'RE PULLING A JEWELRY HEIST.

BUT DON'T FEEL BAD. *I'VE* GOT A MASK ON, TOO. AND WHILE YOU'RE WAITING FOR THE POLICE TO ARRIVE, YOU CAN PONDER THE *PROFUNDITY* OF THAT LITTLE PRONOUNCE-MENT.

THWUNK

WHOK

TOODLES. SEE YOU IN THE FUNNY PAPERS.

THAT CERTAINLY WAS MORE *SATISFYING* THAN GETTING MY BUTT KICKED BY THE SCORPION.

SOME DAYS IT EVEN SEEMS WORTH IT TO HAVE GOTTEN *BITTEN* BY THAT *RADIOACTIVE SPIDER* AND TAKEN ON ITS *ABILITIES.*

IT'S TAKEN A LONG TIME TO REALIZE THAT WITH GREAT *POWER--* THERE MUST ALSO COME GREAT *RESPONSI-BILITY.*

BUT ONCE I DID, I KNEW I HAD TO FIND A WAY TO USE MY POWERS TO *HELP* HUMANITY. AND SO I BECAME A *COSTUMED SPIDER-MAN.*

AND RIGHT NOW, I BELIEVE I CAN HELP *MYSELF* TO A FEW EXTRA *BUCKS* BY SELLING THESE PHOTOS OF SPIDEY IN ACTION--

--TO THE DAILY BUGLE.

PARKER, WHAT'RE YOU TRYING TO *PULL,* BRINGING THESE PHOTOS AROUND HERE?

B-BUT THEY'RE SHOTS OF *SPIDER-MAN,* MISTER JAMESON!

42

YOU'RE DARN *RIGHT* THEY ARE AND THEY MAKE HIM LOOK LIKE SOME KIND OF BLASTED *HERO!*

THESE PHOTOS *DON'T* SHOW HIM AS THE *PUBLIC MENACE* I KNOW HIM TO *BE!*

THE KIND OF PUBLIC MENACE *YOU'VE MADE HIM* OUT TO BE, YOU MEAN!

THESE PHOTOS ARE *NO* DIFFERENT THAN ANY OTHERS I'VE PEDDLED AROUND HERE!

I GUESS I'VE WORN OUT MY WELCOME AROUND THE BUGLE! THAT'S OKAY, BECAUSE I'VE *HAD IT* WITH YOU AND YOUR *PARANOIA* CONCERNING SPIDER-MAN!

YOU'LL *TWIST* THE TRUTH *ANY* WAY YOU CAN IN ORDER TO MAKE HIM LOOK *BAD!* AND I *DON'T* INTEND TO BE A PART OF IT ANY *LONGER!*

HAVE A NICE DAY!

LATER, AS PETER TRUDGES TO HIS HOME IN FOREST HILLS, QUEENS...

WELL, *THAT* WAS A BRILLIANT MOVE, PARKER. I'VE GOT BILLS TO PAY THAT JUST WON'T QUIT--

--SO I CUT OFF MY *ONLY* SOURCE OF INCOME WITH A STUPID OUTBURST! =Yeesh=

OH, WELL. MAYBE LUNCH WITH *MARY JANE* WILL CHEER ME UP.

AFTER LUNCH...

MARY JANE, I DON'T KNOW WHY I CAME TO *YOU* WITH THIS, BUT I TOLD JONAH *OFF* TODAY.

I QUIT. HE COMPLAINED THAT MY SPIDER-MAN PHOTOS MADE HIM LOOK TOO HEROIC. CAN YOU IMAGINE?

ANYWAY, I DID IT. AND NOW I DON'T HAVE A SOURCE OF INCOME! I KNOW YOU CAN'T UNDERSTAND--

PETER, I UNDERSTAND. HE COULD GET UNDER *ANY-ONE'S* SKIN.

I'VE ONLY MET HIM *ONCE*, AND I CAN'T *STAND* HIM. BUT REMEMBER, THE BUGLE ISN'T THE *ONLY* NEWSPAPER IN TOWN.

WHY NOT TAKE YOUR PHOTOS TO THE *GLOBE*?

THE GLOBE?

WHY NOT?

YOU'RE RIGHT. I'M GOING OVER THERE RIGHT NOW.

AND MARY JANE...

...THANKS!

MR. BUSHKIN, THIS IS PETER PARKER WHO PHONED, A FREELANCE PHOTOGRAPHER HERE TO SEE YOU.

I'LL CALL YOU BACK.

BARNEY BUSHKIN HERE, PARKER. I'VE SEEN YOUR WORK IN THE BUGLE. NICE STUFF.

I'M HAPPY YOU'VE BROUGHT YOUR PHOTOS OVER TO THE GLOBE. I'M *SURE* WE'LL HAVE NO TROUBLE RUNNING THEM. WE HAVE NO AXES TO GRIND.

THANK YOU, SIR.

NOW AS FOR MY RATE...

WE'LL *DOUBLE* WHAT-EVER JAMESON WAS GIVING YOU.

MS. DITHERS WILL CUT YOU A CHECK ON THE WAY OUT.

HOPE TO SEE YOU AT THE NEWSPAPER PUBLISHERS AWARDS DINNER TONIGHT. MY TREAT.

44

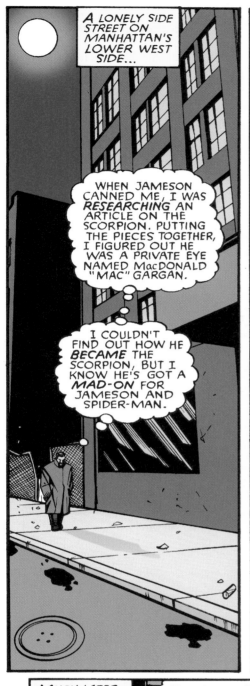

A LONELY SIDE STREET ON MANHATTAN'S LOWER WEST SIDE...

WHEN JAMESON CANNED ME, I WAS *RESEARCHING* AN ARTICLE ON THE SCORPION. PUTTING THE PIECES TOGETHER, I FIGURED OUT HE WAS A PRIVATE EYE NAMED MacDONALD "MAC" GARGAN.

I COULDN'T FIND OUT HOW HE *BECAME* THE SCORPION, BUT I KNOW HE'S GOT A *MAD-ON* FOR JAMESON AND SPIDER-MAN.

MY RESEARCH ALSO LED ME TO BELIEVE THAT HE SEEKS REFUGE IN THE SEWERS IN THIS PART OF THE CITY AFTER A CRIME SPREE.

SO DOWN THE HATCH I GO...

...TO SEE IF I CAN BRING HIM OUT INTO THE OPEN WITHOUT GETTING KILLED IN THE PROCESS.

MUCH LATER...

SEEMS LIKE I'VE BEEN WANDERING IN THIS RATS' PARADISE FOR HOURS-- AND NOTHING.

COULD I HAVE BEEN WR-- huh?

YOU LIKE THE *STENCH* DOWN HERE-- OR JUST GOT A *DEATH WISH*?

45

SIMPLE. BECAUSE I KNOW WHO YOU *REALLY* ARE -- PRIVATE EYE *MAC GARGAN*.

AND IF I DON'T REPORT TO A FRIEND OF MINE IN A FEW HOURS, THAT INFO GOES STRAIGHT TO THE *POLICE*.

SO, I'LL BE SEEIN' YOU AT THE AWARDS DINNER TONIGHT. DON'T FORGET THE TUX.

=Whew= GUESS I WAS *RIGHT* ABOUT HIM BEING GARGAN. IF I WASN'T, I'D BE *DEAD* NOW.

THE PARKER HOME...

IT WAS *WONDERFUL* OF BARNEY BUSHKIN TO INVITE US TO THE PUBLISHER'S AWARD DINNER TONIGHT.

DO YOU THINK THIS OUTFIT WORKS, PETER?

ON YOU, A *POTATO SACK* WORKS.

Y'KNOW JONAH WOULD NEVER HAVE DONE SOMETHING LIKE THIS FOR ME.

I'LL *NEVER* WORK FOR THAT OLD *SKINFLINT* AGAIN.

NEVER SAY NEVER, TIGER.

THE ONLY THING THAT STINKS ABOUT THIS IS THAT *JONAH'S* THE ONE BEING HONORED. GO FIGURE.

I'D BETTER GET CHANGED.

47

THE HYATT HOTEL, TWO HOURS LATER...

NOW THIS IS *MY* KIND OF PARTY.

RIGHT. MAYBE I CAN GET YOU A JOB AS A WAITER HERE.

Uh-oh. THERE'S J.J.J. HIMSELF.

ACT NICE, PETER.

Umm, CONGRATULATIONS ON THE AWARD, Mr. JAMESON.

YES. I UNDERSTAND YOU'VE GONE OVER TO THE GLOBE.

BAD CAREER MOVE.

SEE. WASN'T THAT HARM-LESS?

LIKE A RATTLE-SNAKE BITE.

EVEN IF I GET NABBED BY THE COPS HERE, I'LL BE ABLE TO REVEAL WHO THE SCORPION *REALLY* IS.

THAT SHOULD BUY ME SOME *LENIENCY*. I WOULDN'T MISS THIS FOR ANYTHING.

THANK YOU, ESTELLE. AND MY THANKS TO *ALL* OF YOU WHO GRACIOUSLY BESTOWED THIS AWARD ON ME.

NOW, JUST LET ME SAY A FEW *BRIEF* WORDS ABOUT JOURNALISTIC INTEGRITY...

LADIES AND GENTLEMEN, OUR HONORED GUEST THIS EVENING, PUBLISHER J. JONAH JAMESON.

MUCH, MUCH LATER...

AND IN CONCLUSION, MY FRIENDS...

Oh, BOY.

ZZZZZ

PETER, IS SOMETHING WRONG?

MY SPIDER-SENSE IS GOING OFF. SOMETHING'S GONNA HAPPEN.

49

I DON'T NEED THE CEILING TO FALL IN ON ME TO KNOW THAT--

SKREESH!

--WHAT THE BLUE BLAZES WAS THAT?!

RIGHT ON *TIME!* AND LOOK AT ALL THE RUBES RUN LIKE *RABBITS!*

I LOVE IT WHEN A PLAN COMES TOGETHER.

GET OUT WITH THE OTHERS, MJ! I GOTTA FIND A PLACE TO CHANGE!

SURE HOPE NOBODY CAME INTO THE MEN'S ROOM TO *RETCH* DURING JONAH'S SPEECH!

GOING SOMEWHERE, JAMESON?

THIS IS MY CHANCE. WHILE THE SCORPION'S BUSY, I CAN SPILL THE BEANS ABOUT WHO HE REALLY IS!

THAT KIND OF INVESTIGATIVE REPORTING IS GOING TO PUT FUGITIVE EDDIE BROCK BACK IN THE GOOD GRACES OF THE JOURNALISTIC COMMUNITY.

AND THAT'S ALL YOU'VE GOT TO SAY BEFORE I SNAP YOUR NECK?

≥GLURPH≤ ≥GALPH≤

LISTEN UP, PEOPLE! I'VE DISCOVERED WHO THE SCORPION IS! HE'S MAC GARGAN-- THE PRIVATE EYE!

WHY YOU ROTTEN STOOLIE, BROCK!

RIGHT AFTER I'M DONE WITH BRISTLE HEAD HERE, YOU'RE NEXT!

"BRISTLE HEAD"! THAT'S A GOOD ONE! CAN I USE IT OR DID YOU COPYRIGHT IT, SCORPY?

THWAMM

SPIDER-MAN--HOW?!

NO USE!

NO ONE CAN HEAR ME OVER THE PANIC!

OFFICERS, I WAS *ATTACKED* BY *BOTH* THE *SCORPION* AND *SPIDER-MAN!* THEN THAT WALL-CRAWLING MENACE TURNED ON HIS ACCOMPLICE AND FLED!

THEY WERE OUT TO *RUIN* MY EVENING OF RECOGNITION--

--BUT *FAILED* WHEN I *REFUSED* TO BUCKLE UNDER TO THEIR *THREATS!*

I'LL SOON HAVE *PROOF* THAT SPIDER-MAN AND THE SCORPION *ORCHESTRATED* THIS ENTIRE INCIDENT!

I'LL SOON HAVE *PROOF* THAT THE SCORPION IS, IN FACT, A *CREATION* OF SPIDER-MAN *HIMSELF!*

WHAT A COMPLETE DISASTER.

THE ONLY THING *WORSE* WOULD'VE BEEN IF I'D BEEN CAPTURED BY THE COPS!

GENTLEMEN OF THE PRESS, THIS IS FRONT PAGE NEWS...

...SO SNAP AWAY.

PETER, UNLESS YOU WANT THE GLOBE TO BE SCOOPED...

I HEAR YOU.

THAT'S GREAT, MR. JAMESON. VERY HEROIC.

DO ME IN PROFILE NEXT, PARKER.

THE FOLLOWING DAY...

THANKS AGAIN FOR SENDING ME TO THE DINNER, MR. BUSHKIN.

THE PHOTOS ARE A *BONUS,* HOPE YOU *LIKE* 'EM.

LIKE THEM?

HOW CAN I *LIKE* PHOTOS THAT MAKE MY *MAJOR COMPETITOR* LOOK LIKE A *HERO?*

THIS'LL PROBABLY *INCREASE* THE BUGLE'S CIRCULATION BY FIFTY PER CENT!

I DON'T *INTEND* TO BECOME A *LAUGHING STOCK* IN THE NEWSPAPER BUSINESS!

NOW YOU GET YOUR BUTT *OUTTA* MY OFFICE AND DON'T *EVER* COME BACK!

EVER!

54

THE END.

CREATE YOUR OWN SUPERHERO!

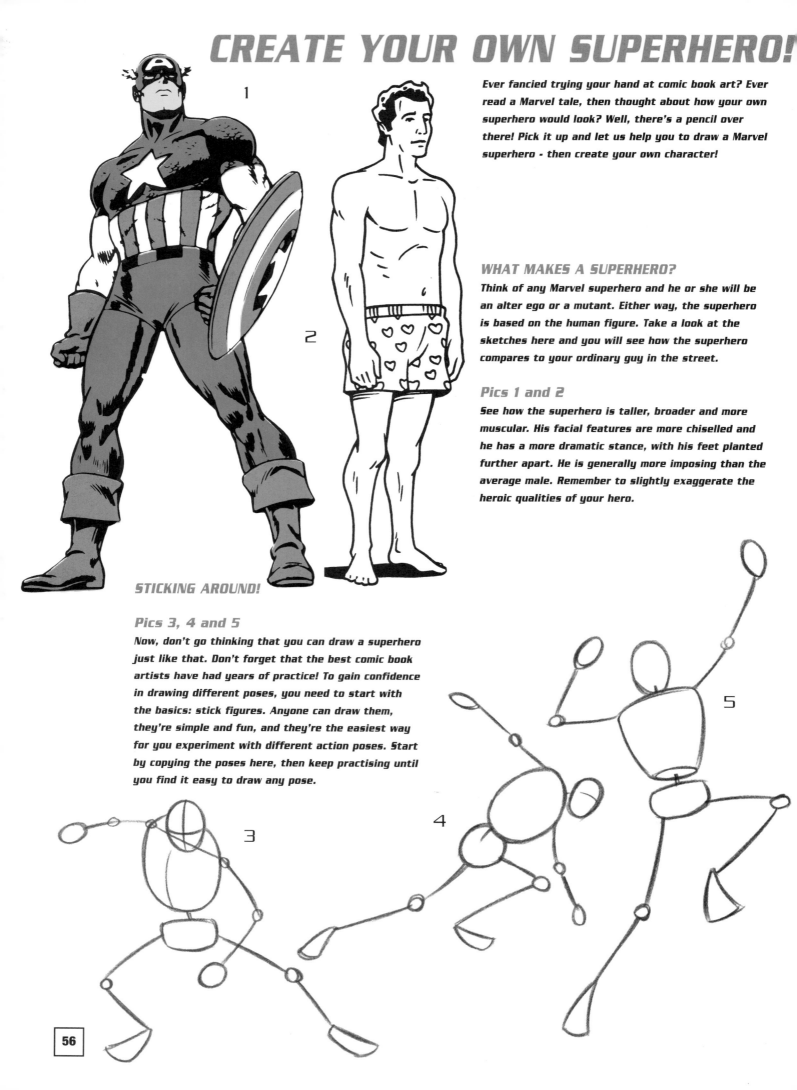

Ever fancied trying your hand at comic book art? Ever read a Marvel tale, then thought about how your own superhero would look? Well, there's a pencil over there! Pick it up and let us help you to draw a Marvel superhero - then create your own character!

WHAT MAKES A SUPERHERO?

Think of any Marvel superhero and he or she will be an alter ego or a mutant. Either way, the superhero is based on the human figure. Take a look at the sketches here and you will see how the superhero compares to your ordinary guy in the street.

Pics 1 and 2

See how the superhero is taller, broader and more muscular. His facial features are more chiselled and he has a more dramatic stance, with his feet planted further apart. He is generally more imposing than the average male. Remember to slightly exaggerate the heroic qualities of your hero.

STICKING AROUND!

Pics 3, 4 and 5

Now, don't go thinking that you can draw a superhero just like that. Don't forget that the best comic book artists have had years of practice! To gain confidence in drawing different poses, you need to start with the basics: stick figures. Anyone can draw them, they're simple and fun, and they're the easiest way for you experiment with different action poses. Start by copying the poses here, then keep practising until you find it easy to draw any pose.

Pic 6

Say you want to draw Spider-Man in an action pose. First use your simple stick figure to get the pose you want, remembering to use ovals for the head, rib cage and hips as before.

FLESHING OUT

Once you've got the hang of stick figures, you can try fleshing them out.

Pic 7 - below

Then build the body by adding cylinders for the arms and legs, and fill in the shoulder and abdomen areas as we've done here. Finish by adding the hands and feet.

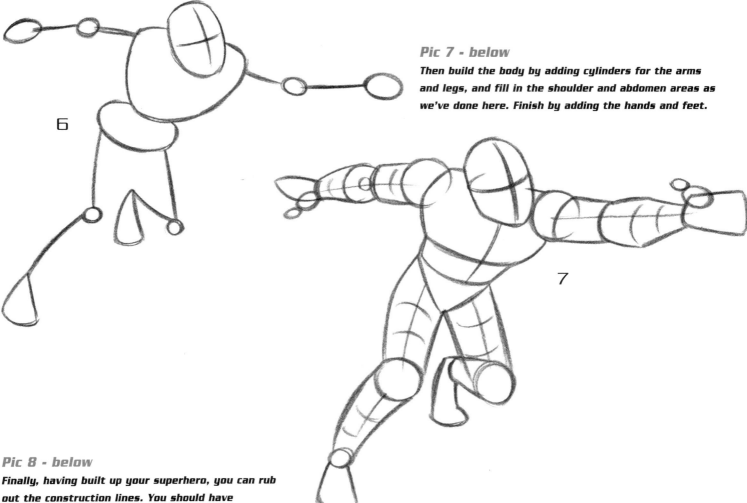

Pic 8 - below

Finally, having built up your superhero, you can rub out the construction lines. You should have something that looks like this pic of Spidey in action!

Of course, that's not all there is to it. To draw like a Marvel master, you need practice, practice and more practice!

Now try creating your own superhero. It's easier if you stay along the lines of the costumed and masked figure, like Spidey. That way, you can stick with the basic figure and not have to worry about facial features. First think up your superhero's name and what his or her special ability will be. Then think about their distinctive costume - what colour will it be? What symbol will it have on it? Ready? Off you go! And keep practising!

57

Profile: Silver Surfer

Norrin Radd lived on the idyllic planet of Zenn-La until he was taken aboard an alien ship headed by Galactus, a supremely powerful being who survived by devouring entire planets. Galactus agreed to spare Radd's planet on one condition: that Radd become his herald to seek suitable planets to nourish him.

Galactus transformed Radd into a silver being that could withstand the rigours of space travel and gave him a unique travel device, enabling him to soar through the vast spaceways of the universe. The Silver Surfer did his duty until Galactus tried to drain Earth of its life-energies. It was then that he rebelled and broke free to use his powers to defend the innocent.

- *Real name:* Norrin Radd
- *Occupation:* Former herald to Galactus
- *Base of operations:* Space
- *Abilities:* Uses his hands to shoot beams of energy which have the destructive force to level a city; rearranges the molecules of matter to create other configurations.
- *Paraphernalia:* Flying 'surfboard' (enables Silver Surfer to travel at almost the speed of light)
- *Height:* 6 ft. 4 ins.
- *Weight:* Unknown
- *Eyes:* White
- *Hair:* None
- *Skin:* Silver

Coming up - the Silver Surfer defends a planet from other predatory space travellers. Read on!

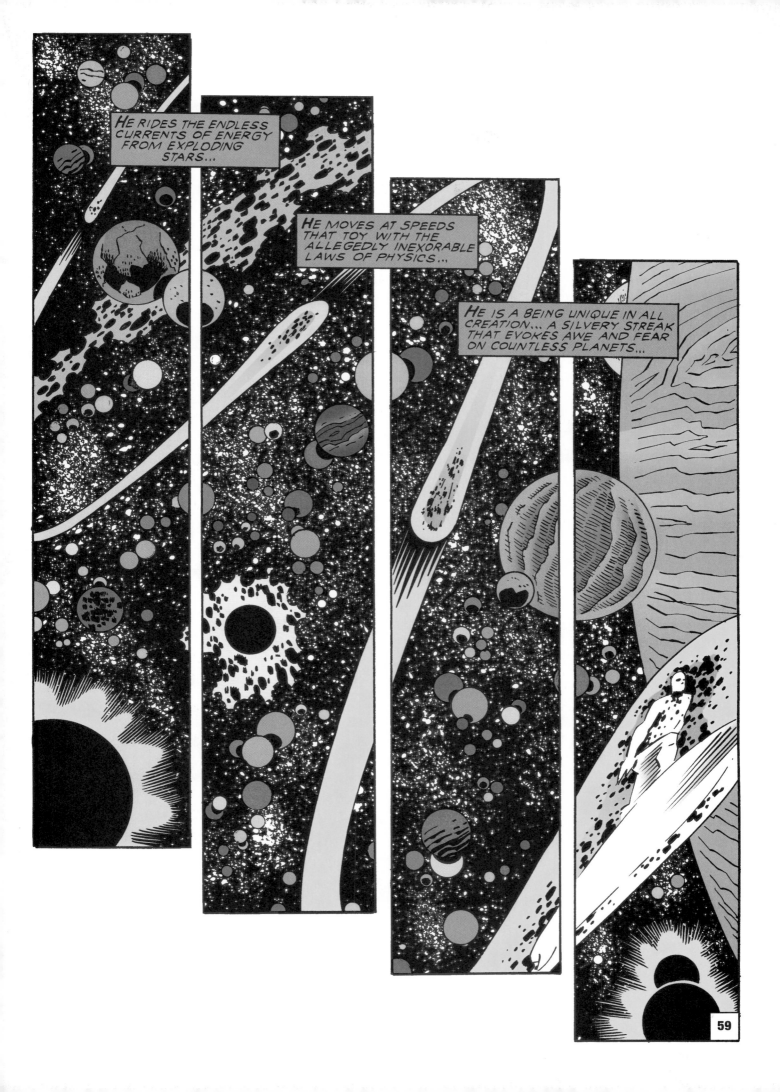

61

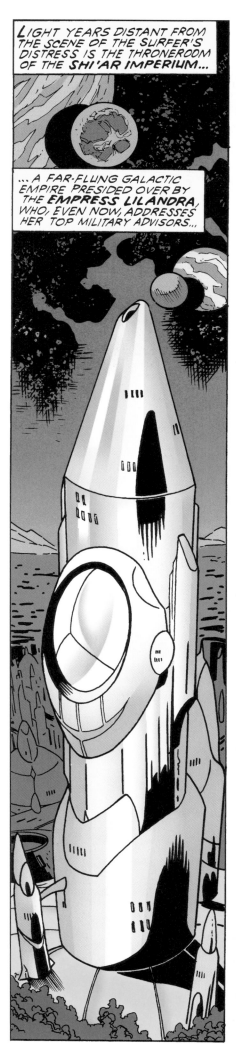

LIGHT YEARS DISTANT FROM THE SCENE OF THE SURFER'S DISTRESS IS THE THRONEROOM OF THE **SHI'AR** IMPERIUM...

...A FAR-FLUNG GALACTIC EMPIRE PRESIDED OVER BY THE **EMPRESS LILANDRA**, WHO, EVEN NOW, ADDRESSES HER TOP MILITARY ADVISORS...

OUR CAMPAIGN INTO THE BARUCCI TWIN SYSTEMS HAS NETTED ANOTHER **DOZEN** WORLDS INTO THE IMPERIUM.

BUT NOW WE FACE PERHAPS OUR GREATEST CHALLENGE-- THE DREADED **BLACK GALAXY** ITSELF!

I AM ORDERING A MILITARY EXPEDITION TO THAT SITE TO ANNEX IT TO THE SHI'AR EMPIRE. QUESTIONS?

WITH ALL DUE RESPECT, EMPRESS, THE BLACK GALAXY IS A VIRTUALLY **UNKNOWN** TERRITORY! WE WOULDN'T EVEN KNOW WHAT TO **PREPARE** OUR FORCES FOR.

I UNDERSTAND YOUR CONCERN, GENERAL.

AND THAT IS WHY I WILL HAVE THE HEAD OF OUR IMPERIAL GUARD-- **GLADIATOR**-- LEAD THE PARTY OF WARSHIPS!

EXCELLENT! HE IS OUR **SUPREME** WARRIOR-- **NEVER** DEFEATED IN BATTLE!

DESPITE THE COUNTLESS *SUCCESSES*, THE IMPERIAL GUARD HAS HAD AT THE FOREFRONT OF THE EMPIRE'S SPECIAL FORCES--

--WE MUST EVER HONE OUR UNIQUE ABILITIES TO HIGHER AND HIGHER LEVELS.

I AM RESTLESS NOW. IT HAS BEEN MANY WEEKS WITHOUT A MILITARY EXPEDITION TO SATISFY MY CRAVING FOR COMBAT.

SKUNKH

ALPHA RAY TRANSDUCER ON AUTO-TARGET HAS ME IN ITS SIGHTS!

A LOW LEVEL DOSE OF *THERMOSCOPIC VISION--*

ZZT

--WILL MELT THE MECHANISM TO SLAG!

STASSSSS

MOMENTS LATER...

AND WITH YOU LEADING OUR FORCES THERE WILL BE VIRTUALLY *NO CHANCE* OF FAILURE. YOUR PRESENCE SERVES AS SUCH INSPIRATION.

INDEED. AND WITH THE EMPRESS'S PERMISSION, WE WILL MAKE THE NECESSARY PREPARATIONS.

GRANTED, GENERAL NEIL FAGIN.

WHILE I *RELISH* THE CHANCE FOR COMBAT, MILADY, I SUSPECT THERE IS *MORE* TO THIS FORAY THAN WHAT YOU TOLD OUR MILITARY LEADER.

YOU ARE MOST PERCEPTIVE. YES, I HAVE HIGH-LEVEL INTELLIGENCE REPORTS THAT INDICATE THE PLANET-KILLER *GALACTUS* MAY HAVE BEEN REPULSED BY WHATEVER LURKS IN THE BLACK GALAXY.

IF WE *DEFEAT* THE MENACE THEREIN, I AM CERTAIN SUCH INFORMATION WOULD REACH GALACTUS--

--AND HE WOULD THINK *TWICE* BEFORE TARGETING A SHI'AR WORLD FOR DESTRUCTION.

AND, FORGIVE MY SAYING, BUT THE *PRIDE* OF THE SHI'AR--AND *YOURS* AS WELL, WOULD ALSO BE ENHANCED THROUGH SUCH A CONQUEST.

PRIDE IS *ALWAYS* A CONCERN IN ANY MILITARY EXERCISE. YOU, AS A WARRIOR, KNOW THAT.

AND *MY* PRIDE AND THE EMPIRE'S ARE ONE AND THE *SAME*.

I MEANT NO DISRESPECT, MILADY. IT IS SIMPLY THAT THE MORE I KNOW OF THE TRUE NATURE OF   MISSION--

--THE BETTER ABLE I WILL BE TO COMPLETE IT. BY YOUR LEAVE, I GO.

WE WILL SPEAK AGAIN WHEN YOU RETURN FROM THE BLACK GALAXY. YOU ARE DISMISSED.

ELSEWHERE IN THE ENDLESS COSMOS...

SHI'AR WARSHIPS ARE CIRCLING THAT PLANET. I WILL INVESTIGATE AND SEE IF IT'S INHABITANTS HAVE BEEN MENACED.

ALTHOUGH THERE APPEARS TO BE PEACE HERE, THERE IS SOMETHING **ODD** ABOUT NO OVERT MILITARY PRESENCE ON THE PLANET.

I WILL DISGUISE MYSELF AS ONE OF THE DWELLERS... USING MY POWER COSMIC TO ALTER MY FORM...

...AND THEN PROBE THE MIND OF ONE OF THE DENIZENS AND SEE WHAT I CAN LEARN OF THE RECENT EVENTS HERE.

IT'S *INSIDIOUS!* THE SHI'AR HAVE *ASSIMILATED* THIS WORLD'S CULTURE TO SUCH AN EXTENT THAT THE PEOPLE'S SENSE OF COLLECTIVE IDENTITY HAS BEEN STOLEN!

THEY ARE NOT TECHNICALLY *SLAVES*-- MORE LIKE UN-THINKING *COGS* SERVING THE GREATER EMPIRE PLACIDLY.

THE SHI'AR WILL *ANSWER* TO THE SILVER SURFER FOR SUCH *REPULSIVE* MIND CONTROL!

67

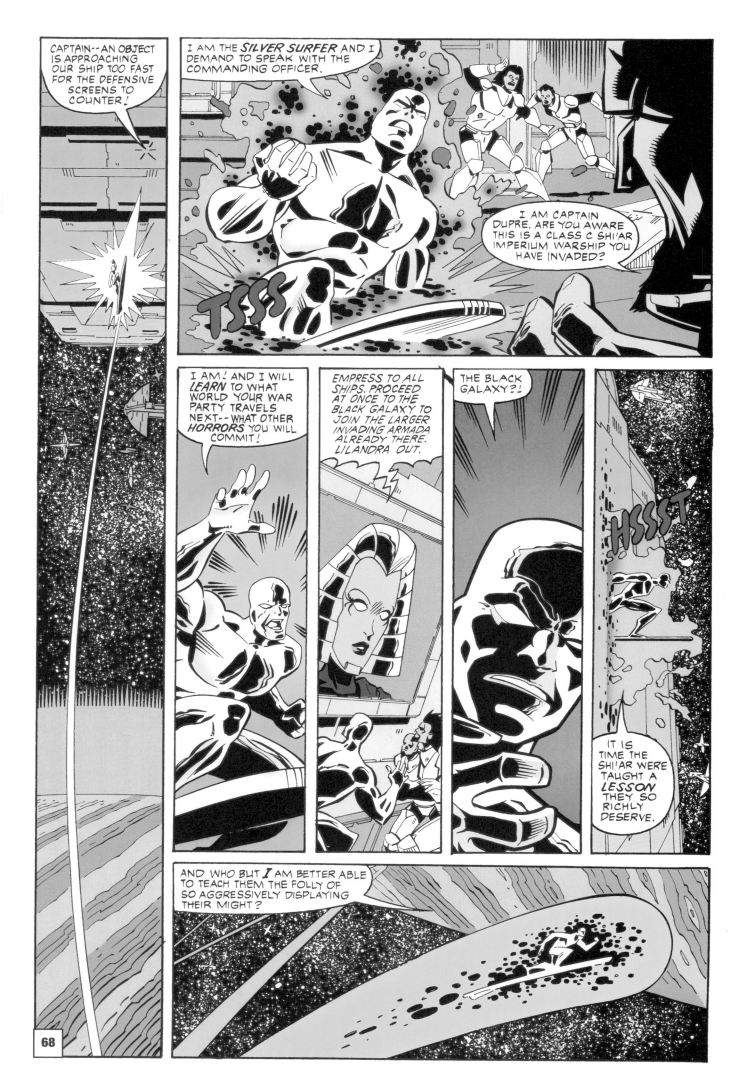

THE EDGE OF THE BLACK GALAXY...

SO FAR, NONE OF THE PROBES WE HAVE SENT WITHIN THIS STRANGE REGION OF SPACE HAVE YIELDED THE SLIGHTEST INFORMATION.

ONCE THEY ENTER, THE TRANSMISSIONS ARE SEVERED.

DO WE DARE PROCEED, GLADIATOR? DO WE DARE ENTER A PLACE WE HAVE NO KNOWLEDGE OF?

WE ARE *SHI'AR!* THERE IS *NO* REGION WHICH IS OFF-LIMITS TO US!

WE HAVE OUR ORDERS FROM LILANDRA HERSELF! *PROCEED!*

THEN, AS THE WARSHIPS CROSS THE THRESHOLD INTO THIS TRULY BIZARRE REGION OF SPACE...

BY THE *EMPRESS'S SCEPTER!* WHAT HAVE WE STUMBLED UPON?

NOT IN *ALL* MY NIGHTMARES COULD I HAVE CONCEIVED OF ANYTHING SUCH AS *THIS!*

EVEN I, IN ALL MY TRAVELS, HAVE *NEVER* SEEN THE LIKE!

73

WHERE OUR ARSENAL FAILS... GLADIATOR MAY SUCCEED!

I WILL HURTLE AT NEAR-LIGHT VELOCITY INTO EGO'S SURFACE WHILE HE IS OTHERWISE OCCUPIED.

BRAMM

WHILE A *SINGLE* BLOW MAY NOT DAMAGE AN ENTITY OF HIS ENORMOUS SIZE...

...*REPEATED* BLOWS WILL WEAR EVEN ONE SUCH AS EGO DOWN!

AND AT THAT MOMENT, THE DRAMATIC FIGURE OF THE SILVER SURFER APPEARS...

WHILE I HAVE THE ELEMENT OF *SURPRISE* ON MY SIDE-- I WILL USE IT TO DISABLE AS MANY WARSHIPS AS POSSIBLE!

BRAKK

WRAKK

SKRASH

PTWASH

THIS SHI'AR ATTACK WILL *CEASE!* NO HARM WILL COME TO EGO -- *NONE!*

YOU HAVE LED THIS WAR PARTY *HERE,* GLADIATOR! YOU WILL LEAD IT *OUT!*

A HARDENED ENERGY COCOON WILL HOLD YOU WHILE WE SPEAK.

TZZZT

I NO LONGER SERVE GALACTUS. NO LONGER AM I HIS "LACKEY" AS YOU PUT IT.

NOW I WILL FOLLOW MY *OWN* CONSCIENCE -- MY *OWN* HEART!

AND THE MAN I AM NOW COULD *NEVER* ALLOW INJURY OR DEATH TO *ANY* UNDESERVING CREATURE! AND I WILL *FIGHT* UNTIL THERE IS NO BREATH WITHIN ME TO *STOP* YOU!

THEN LET THERE BE AN END TO HOSTILITIES! I HAVE NO DESIRE TO SEEK YOUR DEATH, SILVER SURFER.

YOU ARE A NOBLE FOE WHO TRULY BELIEVES IN THE RIGHTEOUSNESS OF HIS CAUSE.

TWASSS

THUS, BY THE POWER VESTED IN ME AS PRAETOR OF THE IMPERIAL GUARD, I CALL OFF THIS ASSAULT ON THE EGO ENTITY.

END

Wolverine's Wordsearch

Heads up, kids! Time to see if you're all payin' attention out there. Hidden in this buncha letters are no less than 24 Marvel comic book words, including the name of yours truly. See how many you can find. Some letters are used more than once and the words read up, down, backwards, forwards, diagonally - every which way! You want a little help? Okay, I'll tell you what the words are, but then you're on your own. Good luck!

WOLVERINE	MUTANT	FANTASTIC FOUR
GAMBIT	SYMBIOTE	THOR
ROGUE	STAN LEE	PUNISHER
STORM	SPIDER-MAN	IRON MAN
BEAST	SCORPION	HULK
CYCLOPS	CAPTAIN AMERICA	DAREDEVIL
X-MEN	HUMAN TORCH	SILVER SURFER
MAGNETO	THING	SUB MARINER

```
B R U O F C I T S A T N A F
G T S H Q R Z C Y C L O P S
H I U Y O T E N G A M W R I
U B B N S P I D E R M A N L
M M M M W F T K L H U L K V
A A A R O H T T Q U E I S E
N G R O L P S Y C R T V C R
T S I T V A X M E N O E O S
O W N S E K J H T T I D R U
R D E B R C S Y N H B E P R
C M R S I I B N A I M R I F
H S T A N L E E T N Y A O E
R O G U E B C O U G S D N R
C A P T A I N A M E R I C A
```

Are You A Marvel Mastermind?

How much do you know about the Marvel Universe? Are you a Marvel mastermind, or bottom of the superhero class? Test yourself with these questions and see how your score rates below! We've given you a choice of answers, so you've at least got a chance of getting a monkey's score!

1 Which superhero appeared on the cover of the first ever Marvel comic book in 1939?
a) Spider-Man
b) The Incredible Hulk
c) The Human Torch

2 Which newspaper does Peter Parker, a.k.a. Spider-Man, work for?
a) The Daily Bugle
b) The Daily Herald
c) The Daily Tribune

3 Whose kid companion was Bucky Barnes?
a) The Punisher's
b) Iron Man's
c) Captain America's

4 Which utopian planet is the Silver Surfer from?
a) La-Zenn
b) Za-Lenn
c) Zenn-La

5 What symbol does The Punisher have emblazoned on his black costume?
a) A scorpion
b) A huge skull
c) A gun

6 Ben Grimm is a member of the Fantastic Four. What is he otherwise known as?
a) The Thing
b) Mister Fantastic
c) The Human Torch

7 Who played The Incredible Hulk in the 1970's TV series?
a) Stan Lee
b) Bill Bixby
c) Lou Ferrigno

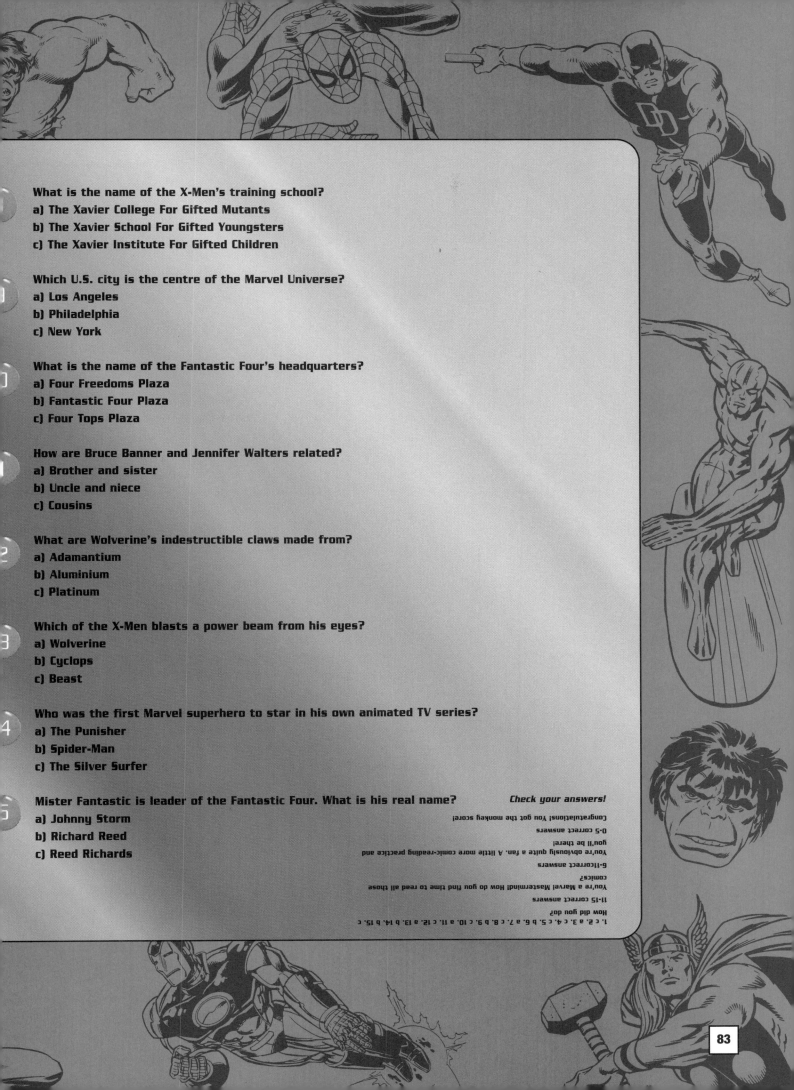

What is the name of the X-Men's training school?
a) The Xavier College For Gifted Mutants
b) The Xavier School For Gifted Youngsters
c) The Xavier Institute For Gifted Children

Which U.S. city is the centre of the Marvel Universe?
a) Los Angeles
b) Philadelphia
c) New York

What is the name of the Fantastic Four's headquarters?
a) Four Freedoms Plaza
b) Fantastic Four Plaza
c) Four Tops Plaza

How are Bruce Banner and Jennifer Walters related?
a) Brother and sister
b) Uncle and niece
c) Cousins

What are Wolverine's indestructible claws made from?
a) Adamantium
b) Aluminium
c) Platinum

Which of the X-Men blasts a power beam from his eyes?
a) Wolverine
b) Cyclops
c) Beast

Who was the first Marvel superhero to star in his own animated TV series?
a) The Punisher
b) Spider-Man
c) The Silver Surfer

Mister Fantastic is leader of the Fantastic Four. What is his real name?
a) Johnny Storm
b) Richard Reed
c) Reed Richards

Check your answers!

How did you do?

11-15 correct answers
You're a Marvel Mastermind! How do you find time to read all those comics?

6-11 correct answers
You're obviously quite a fan. A little more comic-reading practice and you'll be there!

0-5 correct answers
Congratulations! You got the monkey score!

1. c 2. a 3. c 4. c 5. b 6. a 7. c 8. b 9. c 10. a 11. c 12. a 13. b 14. b 15. c

X-MEN

Profile: The X-Men

The X-Men are a group of mutants brought together and trained by Professor Charles Xavier at his School for Gifted Youngsters. Their goal is to protect both humans and mutants from those mutants who would do them harm. They are sworn to defend a world that often fears and hates them.

The X-Men starring in this feature are:

WOLVERINE
- *Real name:* Logan
- *Intelligence:* Superhuman
- *Ability:* Has indestructible Adamantium claws and can regenerate cells at an incredible rate

CYCLOPS
- *Real name:* Scott 'Slim' Summers
- *Intelligence:* Normal
- *Ability:* Can fire a destructive power beam from his eyes

STORM
- *Real Name:* Ororo Munroe
- *Intelligence:* Above normal
- *Ability:* Has the power to control the weather, can fly at subsonic speed (when propelled by winds)

GAMBIT
- *Real name:* Remy LeBeau
- *Intelligence:* Normal
- *Ability:* Can charge any object with explosive kinetic energy, has unbreakable metal legs.

Next! The X-men team up with Spider-man to become a force to be reckoned with in our last Marvel adventure!

STAN LEE PRESENTS: **A LITTLE KNOWLEDGE**

The sleek aircraft descends over the Westchester County mansion housing the Xavier School for Gifted Youngsters.

It is a unique academy wherein those possessing genetically-birthed powers may come to learn to use those abilities...

...use them in the service of a world of ordinary humans that hates them, and if the students succeed, they become... X-Men.

RALPH MACCHIO
WRITER

ANDY KUHN
PENCILER

HARRY CANDELARIO
INKER

KEVIN TINSLEY
COLORIST

MICHAEL HIGGINS
LETTERER

MARK BERNARDO
EDITOR

BOB HARRAS
ED. IN CHIEF

BUT THE MOST BIZARRE THING WAS THE APPEARANCE OF THAT *ALIEN* WHO TELEPORTED AWAY WITH BOTH MAGNETO AND HIS LACKEY, THE TOAD.

YOU ARE RIGHT, CYCLOPS. PERHAPS PROFESSOR XAVIER CAN SHED SOME LIGHT ON THIS SUBJECT.

SPIDER-MAN!

WHAT ARE *YOU* DOING HERE?

I CONTACTED HIM BECAUSE I TELEPATHICALLY DETECTED AN ALIEN PRESENCE AND TRACED IT TO AN ENEMY OF THE WEB-SPINNER'S--

--EDDIE BROCK-- OTHERWISE KNOWN AS THE SYMBIOTE *VENOM.* I BELIEVED SPIDER-MAN HIMSELF MIGHT AID ME BE- CAUSE OF HIS KNOWL- EDGE OF VENOM.

WELL, PROFESSOR, WE SAW WHAT WE BELIEVE WAS AN *ALIEN* IN NEW MEXICO, HE TELEPORTED INTO HULKBUSTER BASE AND MADE OFF WITH MAGNETO AND THE TOAD.

THE ALIEN CALLED HIMSELF *THE STRANGER* AND SAID HE WAS IN THE PRO- CESS OF GATHERING BIZARRE LIFEFORMS FOR STUDY.

PERHAPS THIS IS THE SAME ALIEN PRESENCE I DETECTED AROUND EDDIE BROCK. LET US GO TO THE *WAR ROOM.* THERE IS SOMEONE I NEED TO CONTACT.

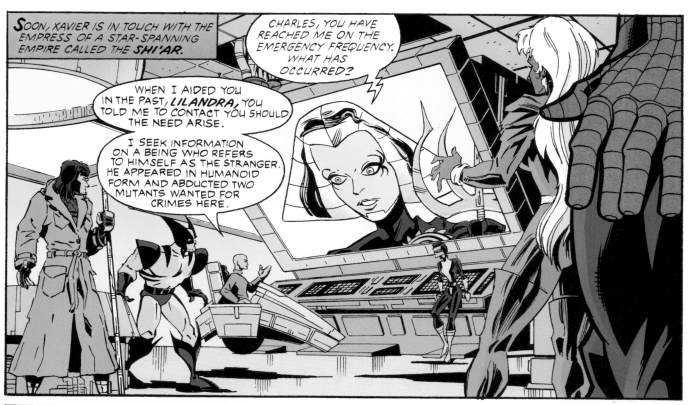

SOON, XAVIER IS IN TOUCH WITH THE EMPRESS OF A STAR-SPANNING EMPIRE CALLED THE *SHI'AR*.

CHARLES, YOU HAVE REACHED ME ON THE EMERGENCY FREQUENCY. WHAT HAS OCCURRED?

WHEN I AIDED YOU IN THE PAST, *LILANDRA*, YOU TOLD ME TO CONTACT YOU SHOULD THE NEED ARISE.

I SEEK INFORMATION ON A BEING WHO REFERS TO HIMSELF AS THE STRANGER. HE APPEARED IN HUMANOID FORM AND ABDUCTED TWO MUTANTS WANTED FOR CRIMES HERE.

THE STRANGER?! HE *IS* KNOWN TO US, CHARLES... PERHAPS THE MOST ENIGMATIC ENTITY IN THE COSMOS. HIS ORIGINS ARE UNKNOWN-- EVEN TO THE SHI'AR.

THE STRANGER IS INTENSELY *CURIOUS.* THINK OF HIM AS A GALACTIC KNOWLEDGE-SEEKER AND SCIENTIST.

HIS DESIRE IS TO KNOW *ALL* THERE IS TO KNOW, AND WOE BE TO *ANY* CREATURE THAT INTERFERES WITH HIS QUEST... FOR HE IS ALSO INCREDIBLY *POWERFUL.*

BE THAT AS IT MAY, LILANDRA, WE *WANT* MAGNETO AND THE TOAD RETURNED TO US. WILL YOU HELP ME?

VERY WELL. I SHALL TELEPORT YOUR X-MEN TO THRONEWORLD, WHERE A CRAFT WILL BE WAITING TO TAKE THEM TO THE STRANGER'S HOME PLANET.

MY THANKS, LILANDRA. JUBILEE WILL REMAIN BEHIND, FOR I NEED HER HERE.

SHORTLY...

I'M NOT MUCH FOR SPACE TRAVEL, BUT IF THE VENOM SYMBIOTE IS INVOLVED, YOU GUYS COULD USE MY EXPERIENCE.

I SALUTE YOUR COURAGE, SPIDER-MAN. FAREWELL.

SHIIINNG

88

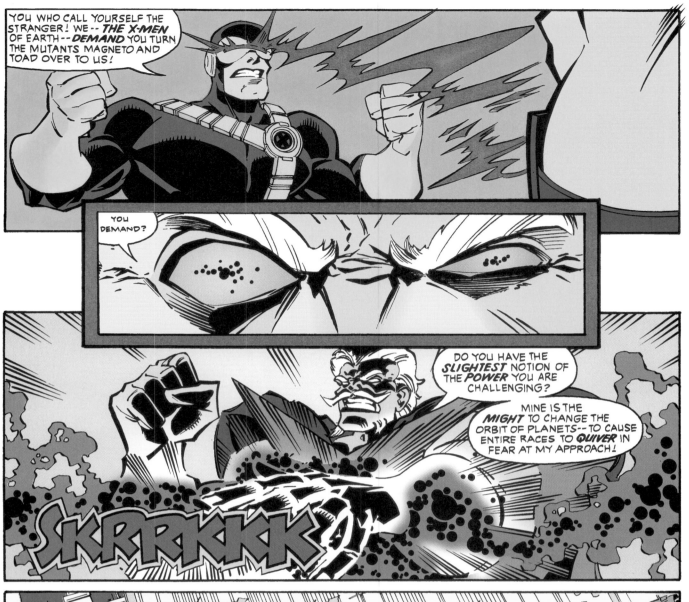

91

92

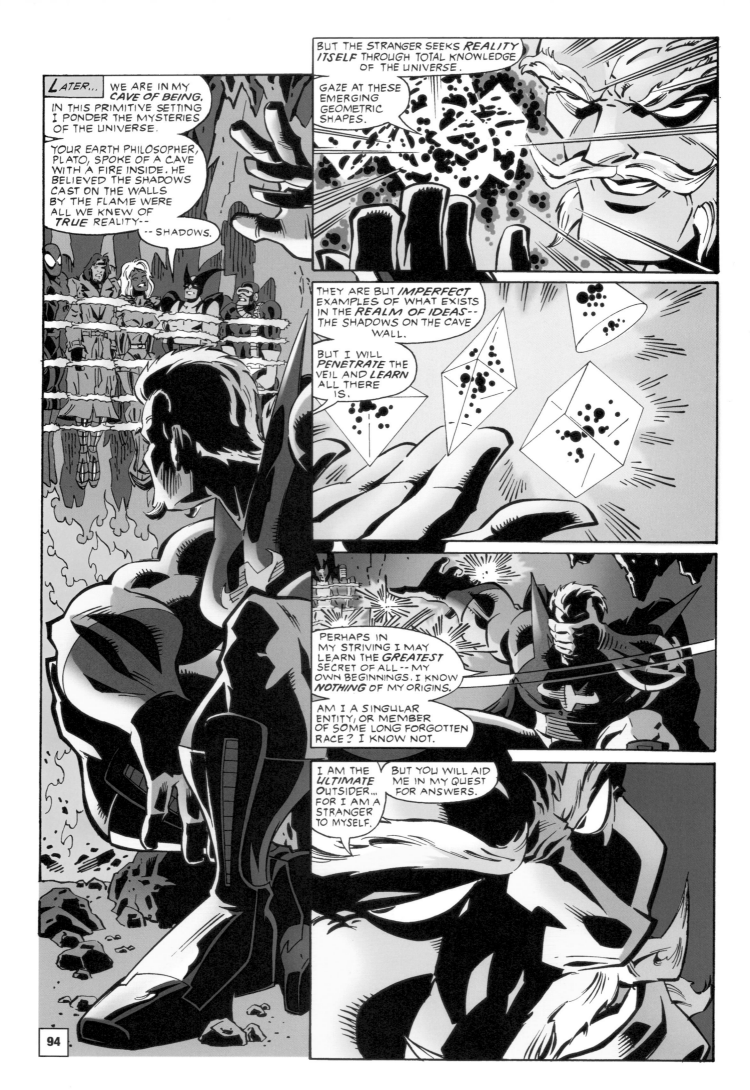

LATER... WE ARE IN MY *CAVE OF BEING.* IN THIS PRIMITIVE SETTING I PONDER THE MYSTERIES OF THE UNIVERSE.

YOUR EARTH PHILOSOPHER, PLATO, SPOKE OF A CAVE WITH A FIRE INSIDE. HE BELIEVED THE SHADOWS CAST ON THE WALLS BY THE FLAME WERE ALL WE KNEW OF *TRUE* REALITY--

--SHADOWS.

BUT THE STRANGER SEEKS *REALITY ITSELF* THROUGH TOTAL KNOWLEDGE OF THE UNIVERSE.

GAZE AT THESE EMERGING GEOMETRIC SHAPES.

THEY ARE BUT *IMPERFECT* EXAMPLES OF WHAT EXISTS IN THE *REALM OF IDEAS*-- THE SHADOWS ON THE CAVE WALL.

BUT I WILL *PENETRATE* THE VEIL AND *LEARN* ALL THERE IS.

PERHAPS IN MY STRIVING I MAY LEARN THE *GREATEST* SECRET OF ALL -- MY OWN BEGINNINGS. I KNOW *NOTHING* OF MY ORIGINS.

AM I A SINGULAR ENTITY, OR MEMBER OF SOME LONG FORGOTTEN RACE? I KNOW NOT.

I AM THE *ULTIMATE OUTSIDER...* FOR I AM A STRANGER TO MYSELF.

BUT YOU WILL AID ME IN MY QUEST FOR ANSWERS.

94

ITS GRIP-- TIGHTENING-- *CHOKING* OFF AIR!

C'MON, LADY! WHAT'RE YOU *WAITING* FOR?

SPIDER-MAN SAID VENOM HAS A WEAKNESS TO INTENSE SOUND. SO I CALL FORTH LIGHTNING AND *THUNDER!*

LET THE *DEAFENING PEALS* SMITE THE CREATURE AND LAY IT LOW!

KRAKA BOOM

ARE YOU *INJURED?*

NEVER BETTER! THAT'S WHAT I CALL *TEAMWORK!* AS SOON AS THE THUNDER WENT OFF HE JUST SHRIVELED UP LIKE A DAISY IN THE DESERT!

SOMETIMES THIS SUPER HERO STUFF IS JUST PLAIN *FUN!*

SHATTERED BY THE INTENSE SOUND, A TELEPATHY-DEADENING DEVICE PLACED ON THE SYMBIOTE'S FOREHEAD BY THE STRANGER *FALLS OFF...*

-- MAY HAVE *DECREASED* THE SYMBIOTE'S CHANCE FOR VICTORY.

...ALLOWING THE ALIEN LIFEFORM TO MENTALLY CONTACT ITS *DISTANT RACE!*

REPLACING THE EARTHLING HOST EDDIE BROCK WITH A HUMANOID *ALIEN* HOST FOR THE ALIEN TO BOND TO--

AGAIN THE EARTHERS DISPLAY THE *VIRTUES* OF COMBINED ASSAULT.

103

AS THEY ENTER THAT WORLD'S ATMOSPHERE, THE SYMBIOTES TRIGGER COUNTLESS WARNING DEVICES...

...BUT THE STRANGER DOES NOT NOTICE.

YOU ARE MINE, NOW!

Eh--? A SHADOW FALLING OVER MY SHOULDER?

SYMBIOTES-- BLACKENING THE SKY!

BACK! THE STRANGER CANNOT FALL TO THE LIKES OF YOU!

LOOK! ABOVE US-- THE SHI'AR SHIP!

I SEE THEM BELOW! PREPARE TO TELEPORT ON MY SIGNAL!

IS THERE NO END TO YOUR NUMBER?

END

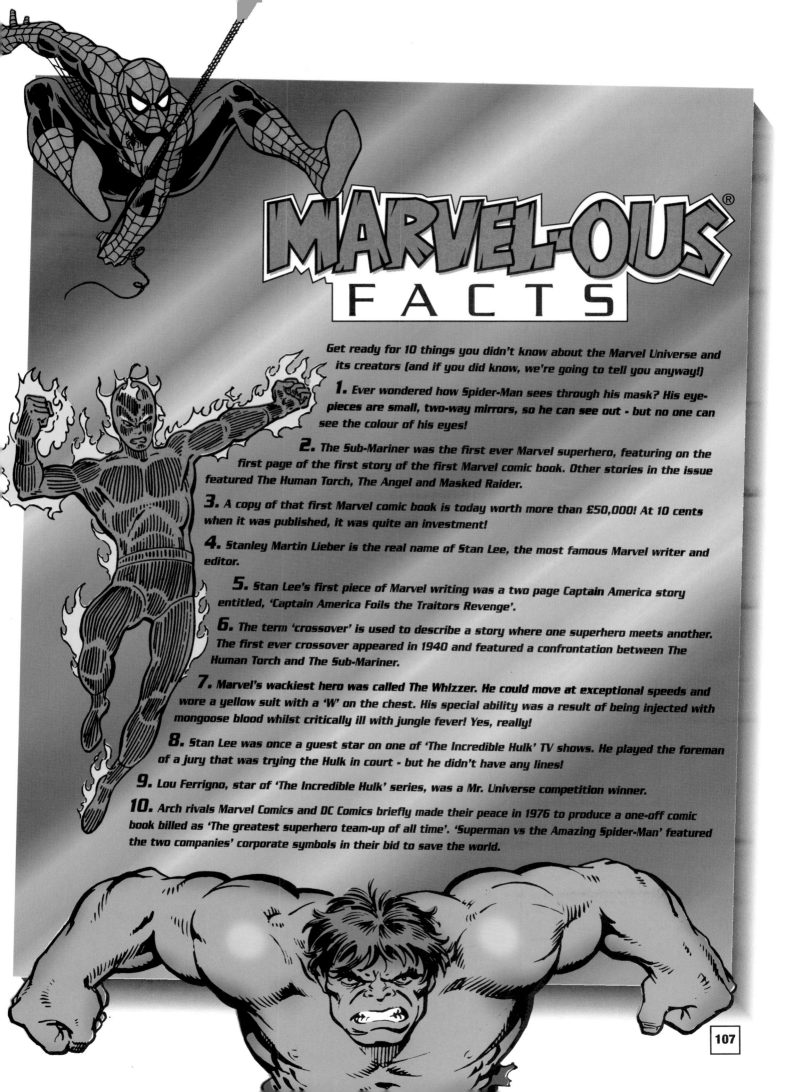

MARVEL-OUS® FACTS

Get ready for 10 things you didn't know about the Marvel Universe and its creators (and if you did know, we're going to tell you anyway!)

1. Ever wondered how Spider-Man sees through his mask? His eye-pieces are small, two-way mirrors, so he can see out - but no one can see the colour of his eyes!

2. The Sub-Mariner was the first ever Marvel superhero, featuring on the first page of the first story of the first Marvel comic book. Other stories in the issue featured The Human Torch, The Angel and Masked Raider.

3. A copy of that first Marvel comic book is today worth more than £50,000! At 10 cents when it was published, it was quite an investment!

4. Stanley Martin Lieber is the real name of Stan Lee, the most famous Marvel writer and editor.

5. Stan Lee's first piece of Marvel writing was a two page Captain America story entitled, 'Captain America Foils the Traitors Revenge'.

6. The term 'crossover' is used to describe a story where one superhero meets another. The first ever crossover appeared in 1940 and featured a confrontation between The Human Torch and The Sub-Mariner.

7. Marvel's wackiest hero was called The Whizzer. He could move at exceptional speeds and wore a yellow suit with a 'W' on the chest. His special ability was a result of being injected with mongoose blood whilst critically ill with jungle fever! Yes, really!

8. Stan Lee was once a guest star on one of 'The Incredible Hulk' TV shows. He played the foreman of a jury that was trying the Hulk in court - but he didn't have any lines!

9. Lou Ferrigno, star of 'The Incredible Hulk' series, was a Mr. Universe competition winner.

10. Arch rivals Marvel Comics and DC Comics briefly made their peace in 1976 to produce a one-off comic book billed as 'The greatest superhero team-up of all time'. 'Superman vs the Amazing Spider-Man' featured the two companies' corporate symbols in their bid to save the world.

MORE MARVEL SUPER HEROES

Here's all you need to know about the rest of the main players in the Marvel Universe!

CAPTAIN AMERICA

Unable to fight for his country in World War II, Steve Rogers volunteered to take part in a government experiment to create a super soldier. His transformation was successful, but the scientist responsible was killed by a Nazi spy before he could continue his work. Thus, the unique Captain America was born and sent out into the world alone to defend the right to freedom.

Real name: Steven Rogers
Occupation: Freelance artist, crimefighter
Abilities: Possesses superhuman agility, strength, speed, endurance and reflexes
Weapon: Indestructible shield

THE PUNISHER

U.S Marine Frank Castle disappeared for months after the murder of his family by mobsters. When he resurfaced, he was armed with an array of sophisticated weapons, determined to get revenge. Discovering that the guilty mobsters were never convicted, he hunted them down and killed them. Dubbed 'The Punisher', he has devoted his life to fighting crime and protecting the innocent.

Real name: Frank Castle
Occupation: Former Marine turned vigilante
Abilities: Excellent marksman and hand-to-hand combatant
Weapons: Entire arsenal of portable weaponry

IRON MAN

Enterprising inventor and munitions expert Tony Stark was taken prisoner by guerrilla fighters during a weapons-testing trip to the Far East. Whilst in captivity, he invented an electrically powered, transistorised suit of armour equipped with mind-boggling weapons. He used it to escape and returned home to found the crime-fighting group, The Avengers.

Real name: Anthony Stark
Occupation: Inventor, industrialist
Abilities: Extensive knowledge of offensive weaponry
Weapon: Indestructible body armour

THE MIGHTY THOR

At the age of sixteen, Thor was presented with a mystic uru hammer by his father, Odin. The hammer can be lifted only by those deemed worthy of its power and is an indestructible throwing weapon that always returns to the spot from which it is thrown after striking its target. On reaching earth as its guardian, Thor discovered the hammer could also control thunder storms.

Real name: Thor
Occupation: Warrior, adventurer
Abilities: Possesses superhuman strength, endurance and resistance to injury.
Weapon: Enchanted hammer

DAREDEVIL

Whilst trying to save a blind man, Matthew Murdock was hit by a truck and himself blinded by leakage from its radioactive load. He soon discovered that his other senses had been dramatically heightened, and later decided to put them to good use to avenge his father's murder. Naming himself Daredevil, he went on to become one of the most famous costumed vigilantes of all time.

Real name: Matthew Michael Murdock
Occupation: Lawyer turned crimefighter
Abilities: Has heightened sense of touch, smell, hearing and taste.
Weapon: Billy club

THE SENSATIONAL SHE-HULK

Jennifer Walters was a successful Los Angeles lawyer and the cousin of Dr. Bruce Banner (a.k.a. The Incredible Hulk). During one of Bruce's visits, Jennifer was shot by a hit man hired by a criminal she was prosecuting. Banner improvised an emergency blood transfusion at the scene, but his gamma-radiated blood turned her into the female version of the legendary Incredible Hulk!

Real name: Jennifer Walters
Occupation: Criminal lawyer, professional adventurer
Abilities: Has superhuman strength and high degree of resistance to pain, injury and disease
Weapon: None